THE EASY CLASSICAL FAKE BOOK

Melody, Lyrics and Simplified Chords

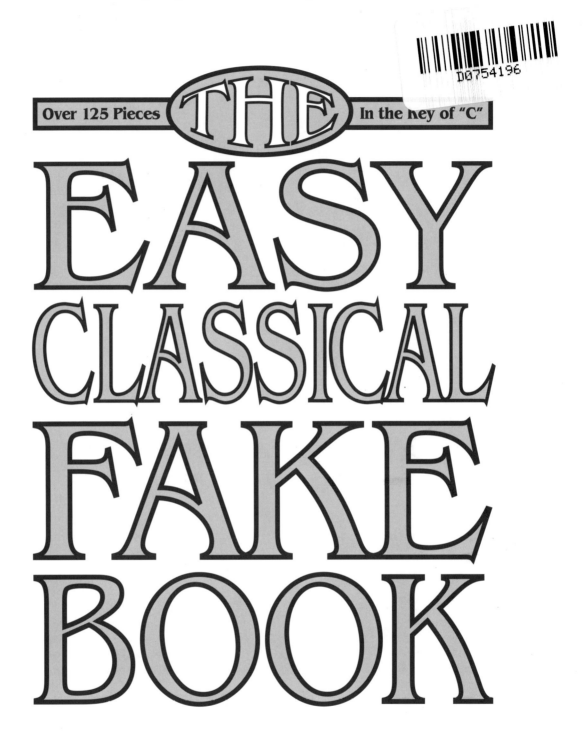

Over 125 Pieces · **THE** · In the key of "C"

EASY CLASSICAL FAKE BOOK

ISBN 1-4234-0156-5

HAL•LEONARD®
CORPORATION

7777 W. BLUEMOUND RD. P.O. BOX 13819 MILWAUKEE, WI 53213

In Australia Contact:
Hal Leonard Australia Pty. Ltd.
4 Lentara Court
Cheltenham, Victoria, 3192 Australia
Email: ausadmin@halleonard.com

Visit Hal Leonard Online at
www.halleonard.com

THE EASY CLASSICAL FAKE BOOK

CONTENTS BY COMPOSER

THE EASY CLASSICAL FAKE BOOK
ALPHABETICAL CONTENTS

INTRODUCTION

What Is a Fake Book?

A fake book has one-line music notation consisting of melody, lyrics and chord symbols. This lead sheet format is a "musical shorthand" which is an invaluable resource for all musicians—hobbyists to professionals.

Here's how *The Easy Classical Fake Book* differs from most standard fake books:

- All songs are in the key of C, which makes them easy to play.

- Many of the melodies have been simplified.

- Only five basic chord types are used—major, minor, seventh, diminished and augmented.

- The music notation is larger for ease of reading.

In the event that you haven't used chord symbols to create accompaniment, or your experience is limited, a chord speller chart is included at the back of the book to help you get started.

Have fun!

DONA NOBIS PACEM
Canon

Anonymous

Moderato

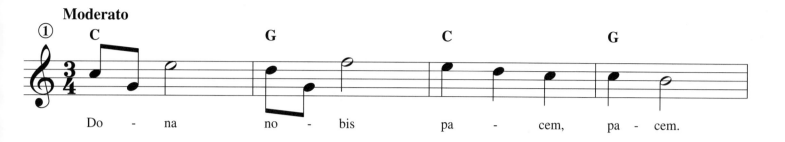

Do - na no - bis pa - cem, pa - cem.

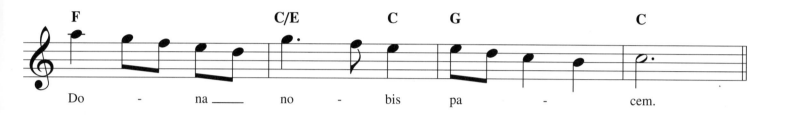

Do - na ____ no - bis pa - cem.

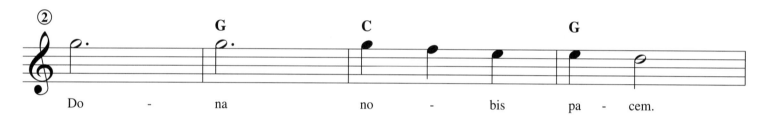

Do - na no - bis pa - cem.

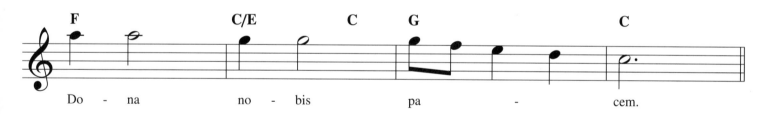

Do - na no - bis pa - cem.

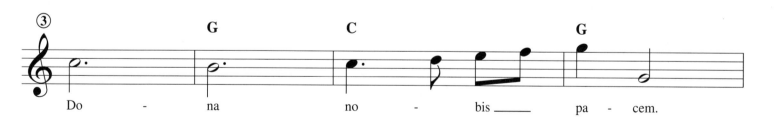

Do - na no - bis ____ pa - cem.

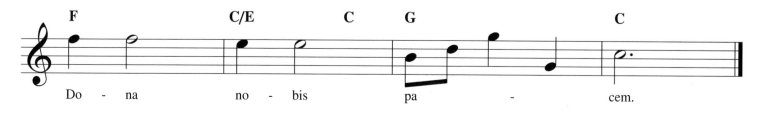

Do - na no - bis pa - cem.

ARIOSO

JOHANN SEBASTIAN BACH

Adagio

GAVOTTE
from *French Suite No. 5*

JOHANN SEBASTIAN BACH

MINUET I
from *The Anna Magdalena Notebook*

JOHANN SEBASTIAN BACH

MINUET II
from *The Anna Magdalena Notebook*

JOHANN SEBASTIAN BACH

Animato

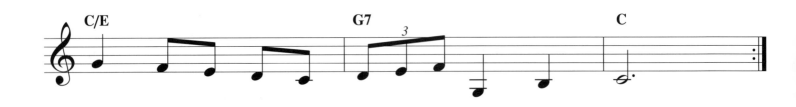

JESU, JOY OF MAN'S DESIRING

JOHANN SEBASTIAN BACH

FÜR ELISE

LUDWIG VAN BEETHOVEN

MINUET II
from *Six Minuets*

LUDWIG VAN BEETHOVEN

Allegretto

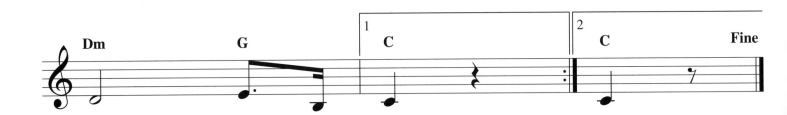

Trio

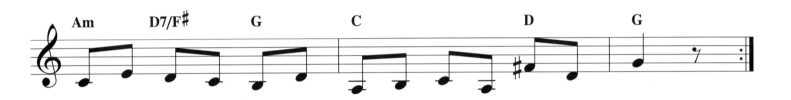

TURKISH MARCH
from *The Ruins of Athens*

LUDWIG VAN BEETHOVEN

SYMPHONY NO. 9
Fourth Movement Theme ("Ode to Joy")

LUDWIG VAN BEETHOVEN

Allegro assai

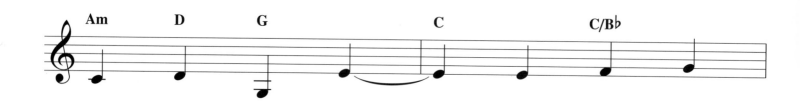

TOREADOR SONG
from *Carmen*

GEORGES

Allegro moderato

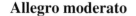

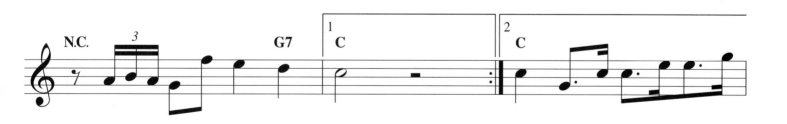

FARANDOLE
from *L'Arlésienne*

GEORGES BIZET

HABANERA
from *Carmen*

GEORGES BIZET

Allegretto quasi andantino

SEGUIDILLA
from *Carmen*

GEORGES BIZET

Allegretto

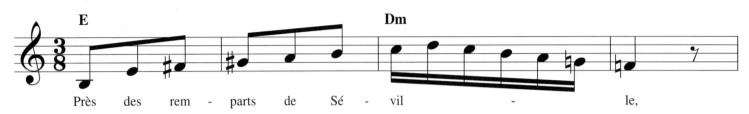

Près des rem - parts de Sé - vil - le,

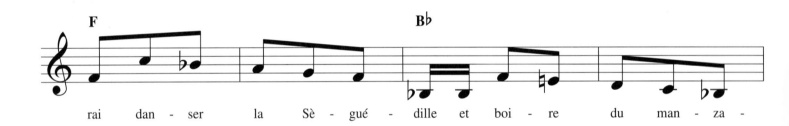

chez _____ mon a - mi _____ Lil - las Pas - tia, _____ j'i -

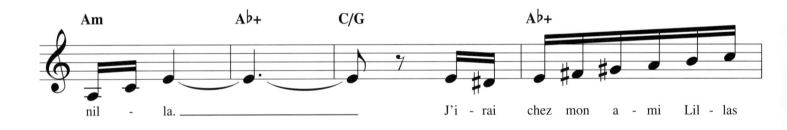

rai dan - ser la Sè - gué - dille et boi - re du man - za -

nil - la. _____ J'i - rai chez mon a - mi Lil - las

Pas - tia.

Oui, mais tou - te seule on s'en - nui - e, et les vrais plai - sirs

sont à deux; donc, pour me te - nir com - pa - gni - e, j'em -

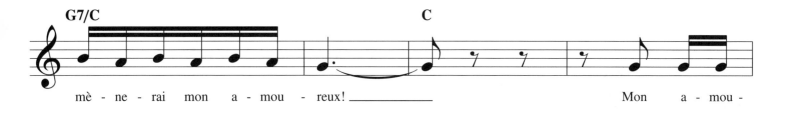

mè - ne - rai mon a - mou - reux! _____ Mon a - mou -

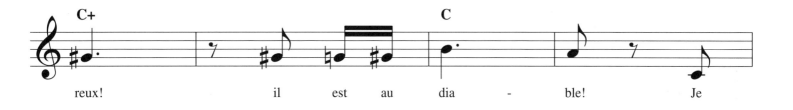

reux! il est au dia - ble! Je

l'ai mis à la por - te hier! Mon _____ pau - vre cœur,

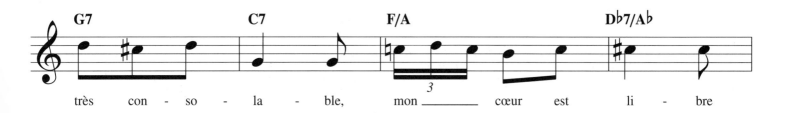

très con - so - la - ble, mon _____ cœur est li - bre

com - me l'air! J'ai des ga-lants à la dou-zai-ne,

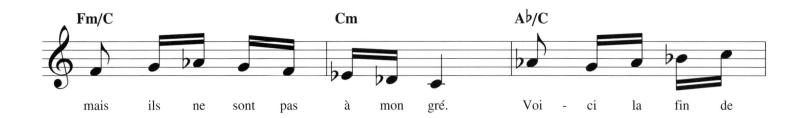

mais ils ne sont pas à mon gré. Voi - ci la fin de

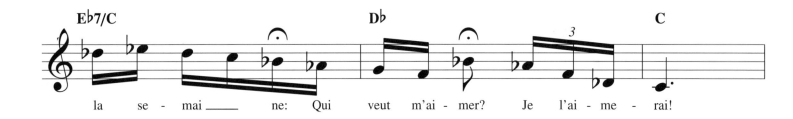

la se - mai____ ne: Qui veut m'ai-mer? Je l'ai-me-rai!

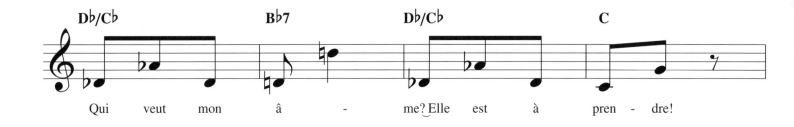

Qui veut mon â - me? Elle est à pren - dre!

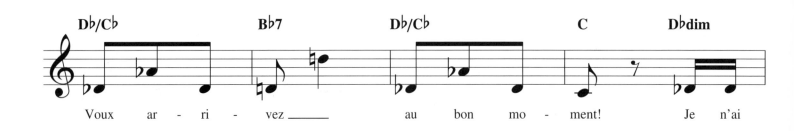

Voux ar - ri - vez____ au bon mo - ment! Je n'ai

guè - re le temps d'at - ten - dre, car a - vec mon nou - vel a -

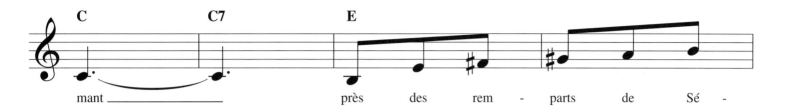

mant _____ près des rem - parts de Sé -

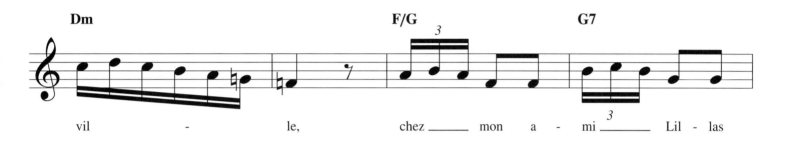

vil - le, chez ___ mon a - mi ___ Lil - las

Pas - tia, _____ nous dan - se - rons la Sé - gué -

dille et boi - rons du man - za - nil - la: _____

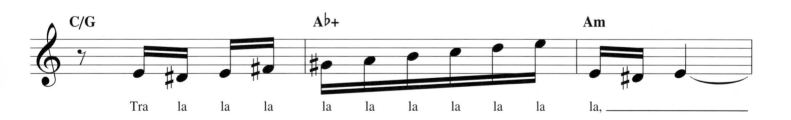

Tra la la la la la la la la la la, _____

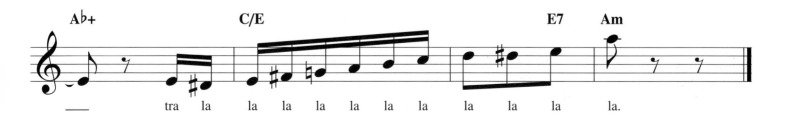

___ tra la la la la la la la la la la la la.

MINUET
from *String Quintet*

LUIGI BOCCHERINI

Allegretto grazioso

FIRST THEME FROM POLOVETZIAN DANCES

from *Prince Igor*

ALEXANDER BORODIN

SYMPHONY NO. 1
Fourth Movement Theme

JOHANNES BRAHMS

Allegro non troppo, ma con brio

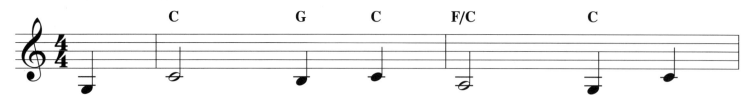

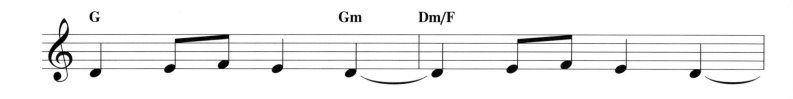

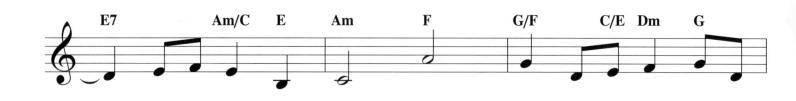

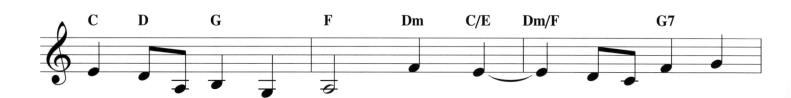

33

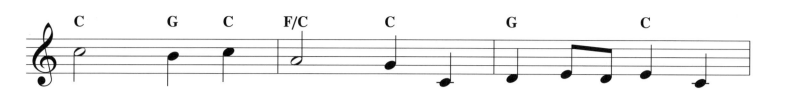

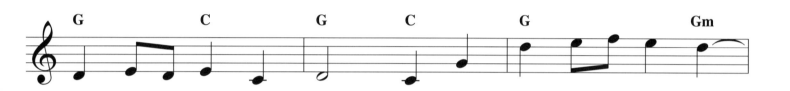

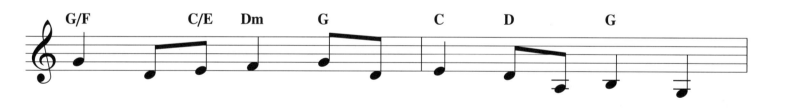

LULLABY

JOHANNES BRAHMS

Dolce, con moto

LONDONDERRY AIR

British Folksong

Lento espressivo

Would God   I   were   the ten - der ap - ple blos - som ___ That floats and
Yea, would to God   I   were a - mong the ros - es ___ That lean to

falls   from off the twist - ed   bough, ___ To lie and faint with - in your silk - en
kiss   you as you flow be - tween, ___ While on the low - est branch a bud un -

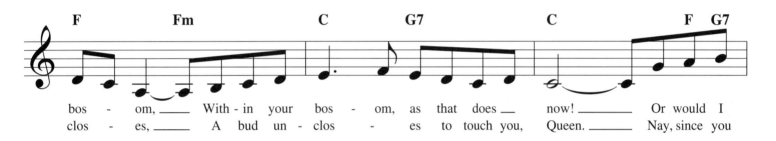

bos - om, ___ With - in your bos - om, as that does ___ now! ___ Or would I
clos - es, ___ A bud un - clos - es to touch you, Queen. ___ Nay, since you

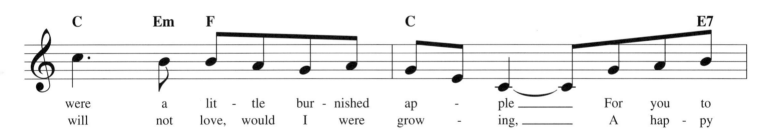

were   a   lit - tle bur - nished ap - ple ___ For you to
will   not love, would I   were grow - ing, ___ A hap - py

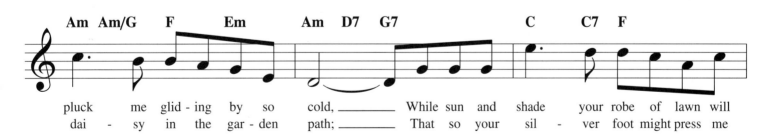

pluck   me glid - ing by so   cold, ___ While sun and shade   your robe of lawn will
dai - sy in the gar - den path; ___ That so your sil - ver foot might press me

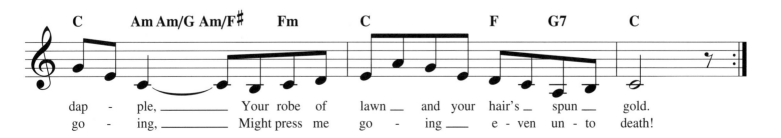

dap - ple, ___ Your robe of   lawn ___ and your hair's ___ spun ___ gold.
go - ing, ___ Might press me   go - ing ___ e - ven un - to death!

FUNERAL MARCH

FRYDERYK CHOPIN

Lento

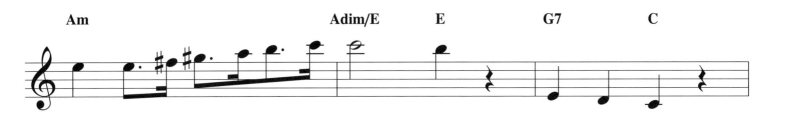

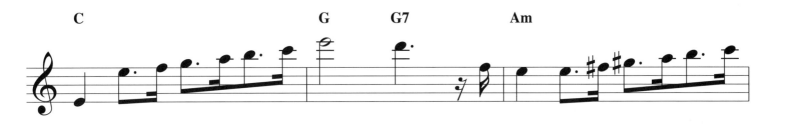

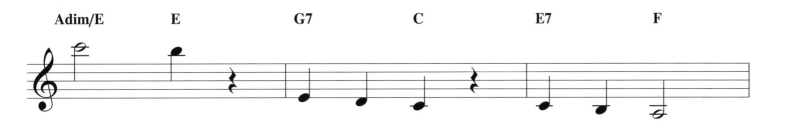

NOCTURNE, Op. 15, No. 3

FRYDERYK CHOPIN

Lento

FANTAISIE-IMPROMPTU

FRYDERYK CHOPIN

PRELUDE, OP. 28, NO. 4

FRYDERYK CHOPIN

PRELUDE, OP. 28, NO. 7

FRYDERYK CHOPIN

Andantino

PRELUDE, OP. 28, NO. 20

FRYDERYK CHOPIN

Largo

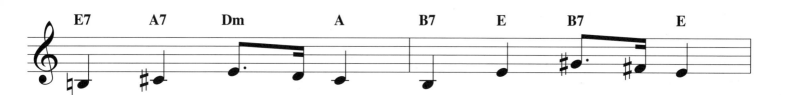

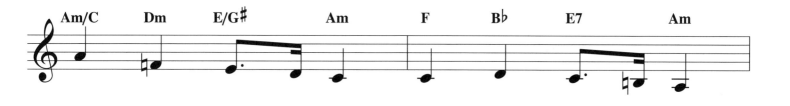

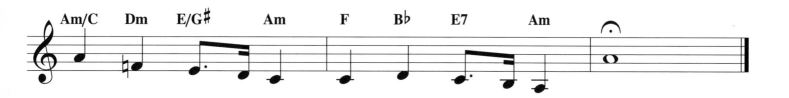

TRUMPET VOLUNTARY

JEREMIAH CLARKE

SONATINA, OP. 36, NO. 1
First Movement Opening

MUZIO CLEMENTI

Allegro

SANTA LUCIA

TEODORO COTTRAU

Moderately

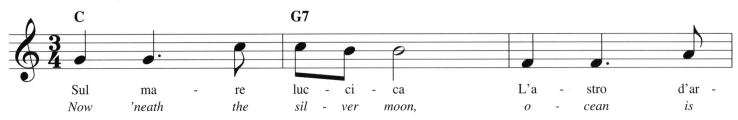

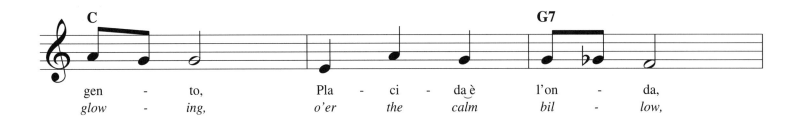

Sul ma - re luc - ci - ca, L'a - stro d'ar -
Now 'neath the sil - ver moon, o - cean is

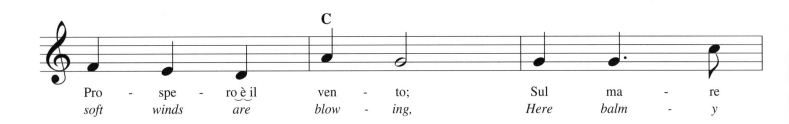

gen - to, Pla - ci - da è l'on - da,
glow - ing, o'er the calm bil - low,

Pro - spe - ro è il ven - to; Sul ma - re
soft winds are blow - ing, Here balm - y

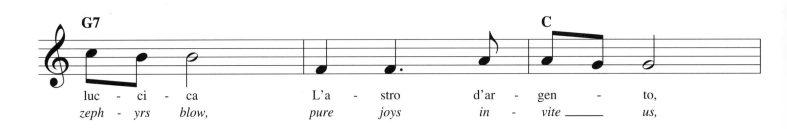

luc - ci - ca L'a - stro d'ar - gen - to,
zeph - yrs blow, pure joys in - vite ____ us,

Pla - ci - da è l'on - da, Pro - spe - ro è il ven - to;
and as we gen - tly row, all things de - light us,

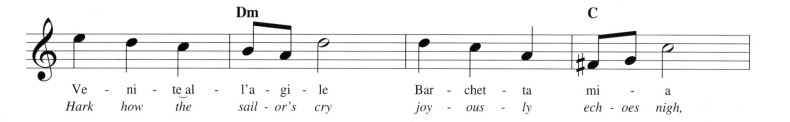

Ve - ni - te al - l'a - gi - le Bar - chet - ta mi - a
Hark how the sail - or's cry joy - ous - ly ech - oes nigh,

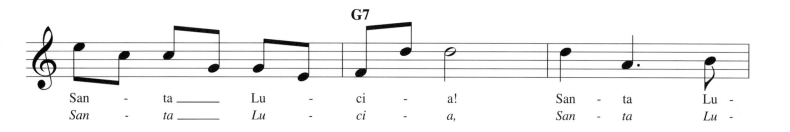

San - ta _____ Lu - ci - a! San - ta Lu -
San - ta _____ Lu - ci - a, San - ta Lu -

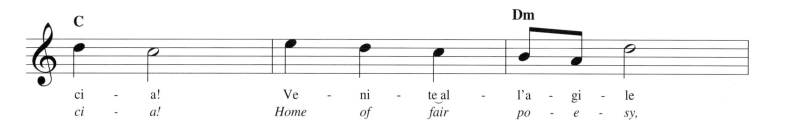

ci - a! Ve - ni - te al - l'a - gi - le
ci - a! Home of fair po - e - sy,

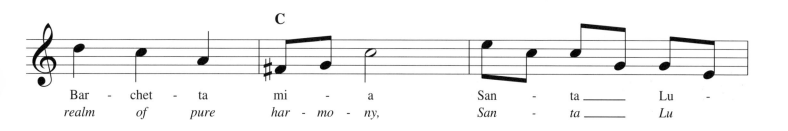

Bar - chet - ta mi - a San - ta _____ Lu -
realm of pure har - mo - ny, San - ta _____ Lu

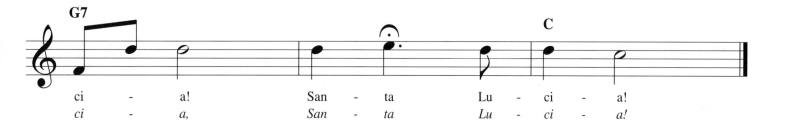

ci - a! San - ta Lu - ci - a!
ci - a, San - ta Lu - ci - a!

RONDO

FRANÇOIS COUPERIN

COME BACK TO SORRENTO

ERNESTO DE CURTIS

COME AGAIN, SWEET LOVE

JOHN DOWLAND

REVERIE

CLAUDE DEBUSSY

Slowly, with expression

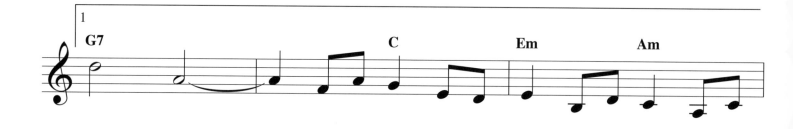

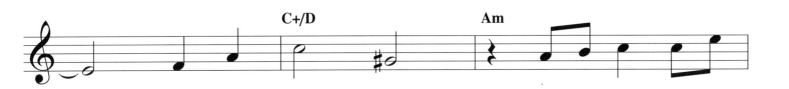

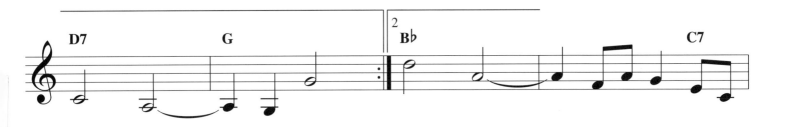

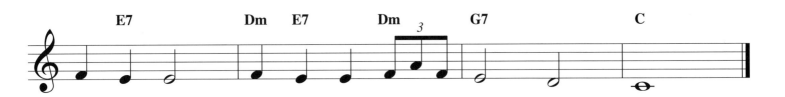

'O SOLE MIO

E. DI CAPUA

Moderately slow

Che bel - la co - sa 'na iur - na - ta'e
Be - hold the bril - liant sun in all its

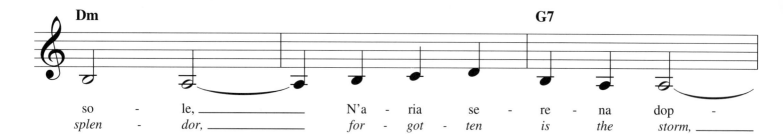

so - le, _____ N'a - ria se - re - na dop -
splen - dor, _____ for - got - ten is the storm, _____

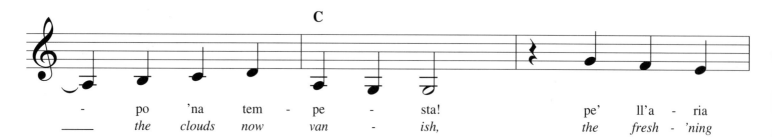

____ - po 'na tem - pe - sta! pe' ll'a - ria
____ the clouds now van - ish, the fresh - 'ning

fre - sca pa - re già 'na fe - sta, _____
breez - es heav - y airs will ban - ish, _____

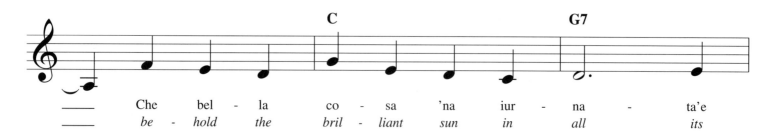

____ Che bel - la co - sa 'na iur - na - ta'e
____ be - hold the bril - liant sun in all its

sole. _____ Ma n'a - tu so - le
splen - dor! A sun I know of

cchiù bel - lo, ohi - ne',
that's bright - er still,

'o so - le
this sun, my

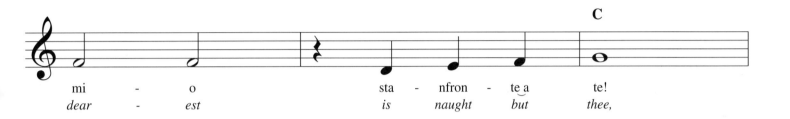

mi - o
dear - est

sta - nfron - te a te!
is naught but thee,

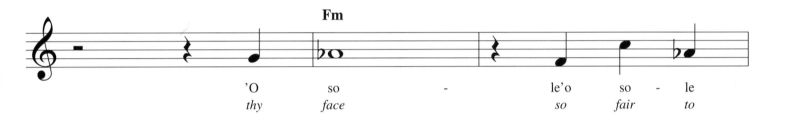

'O so - le 'o so - le
thy face so fair to

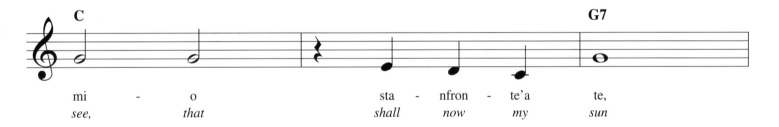

mi - o
see,

sta - nfron - te 'a te,
that shall now my sun

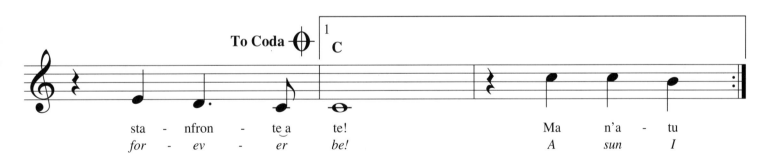

To Coda

sta - nfron - te a te!
for - ev - er be!

Ma n'a - tu
A sun I

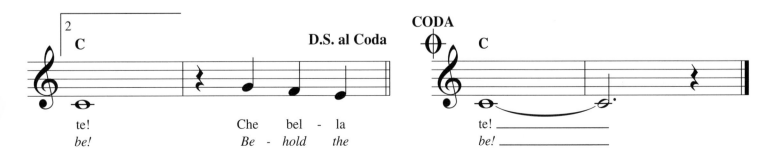

D.S. al Coda

te!
be!

Che bel - la
Be - hold the

CODA

te! _____
be! _____

HUMORESQUE

ANTONÍN DVOŘÁK

Moderately

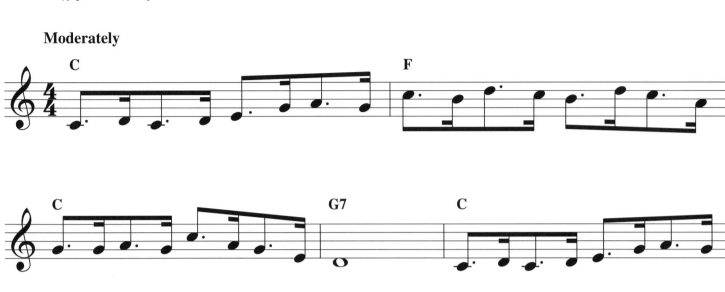

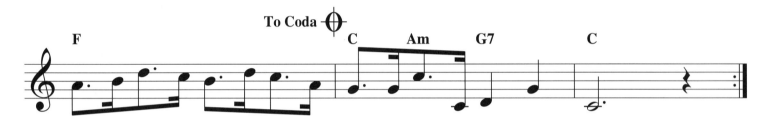

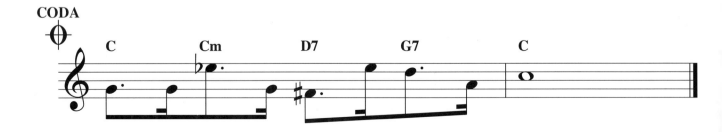

SYMPHONY NO. 9 ("FROM THE NEW WORLD")
Second Movement Theme

ANTONÍN DVOŘÁK

SPINNING SONG

JOHANN ELLMENREICH

THE PALMS

JEAN-BAPTISTE FAURÉ

Andante maestoso

O'er all the way, green palms and blos - soms gay   Are strewn this day in fes - tal

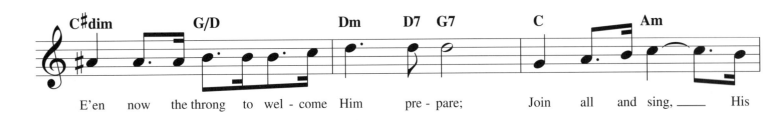

prep - a - ra - tion;   Where Je - sus comes to wipe our tears a - way,

E'en now the throng to wel - come Him pre - pare;   Join all and sing, ___ His

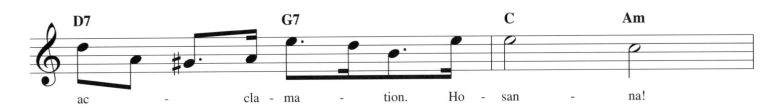

name ___ de - clare,   Let ev - 'ry voice re - sound ___ with

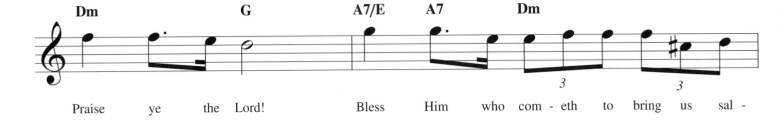

ac - cla - ma - tion.   Ho - san - na!

Praise ye the Lord!   Bless Him who com - eth to bring us sal -

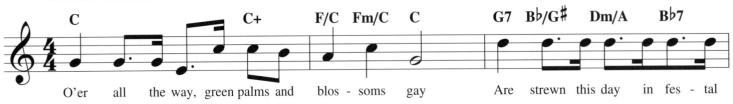

va - tion.

PAVANE

Gabriel Fauré

Andante

SICILIENNE

GABRIEL FAURÉ

Allegretto molto moderato

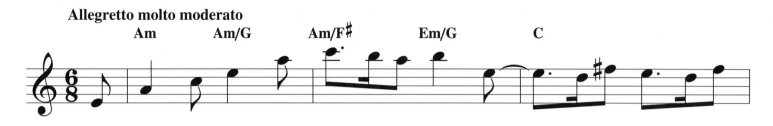

CIELITO LINDO

C. FERNANDEZ

Allegro

Chorus

THE SILVER SWAN

ORLANDO GIBBONS

Lento

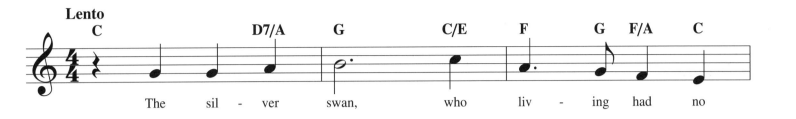

The sil - ver swan, who liv - ing had no

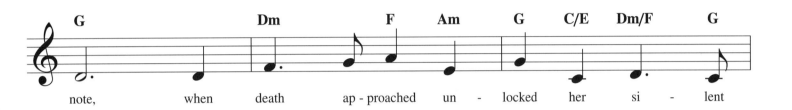

note, when death ap - proached un - locked her si - lent

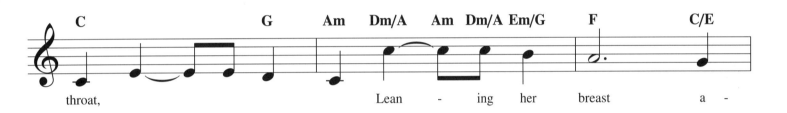

throat, Lean - ing her breast a -

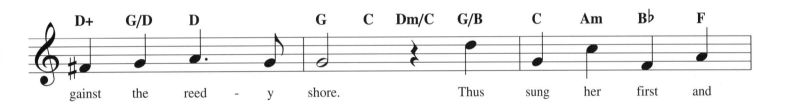

gainst the reed - y shore. Thus sung her first and

last, and ___ sung no more. Fare - well, all

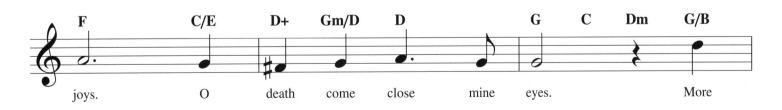

joys. O death come close mine eyes. More

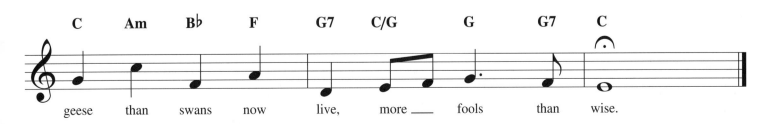

geese than swans now live, more ___ fools than wise.

PANIS ANGELICUS

CÉSAR FRANCK

Poco lento

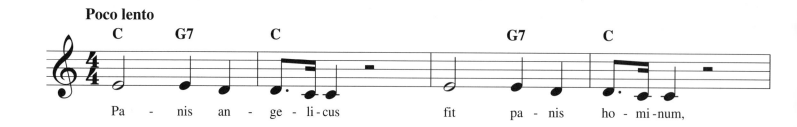

Pa - nis an - ge - li - cus fit pa - nis ho - mi - num,

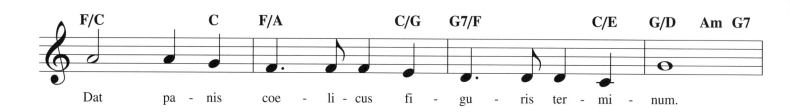

Dat pa - nis coe - li - cus fi - gu - ris ter - mi - num.

O res mi - ra - bi - lis man - du - cat Do - mi - num,

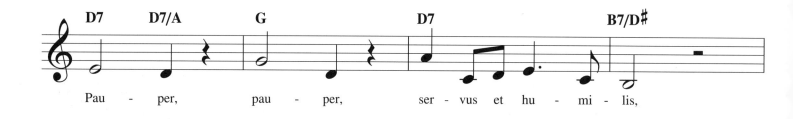

Pau - per, pau - per, ser - vus et hu - mi - lis,

Pau - per, pau - per, ser - vus et hu - mi -

lis.

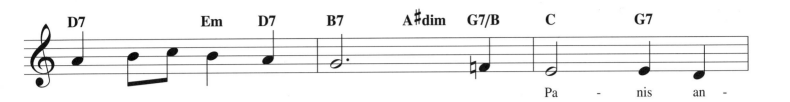

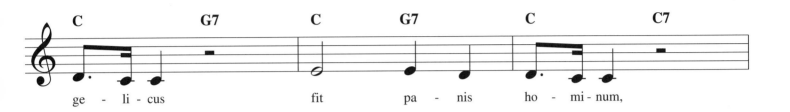

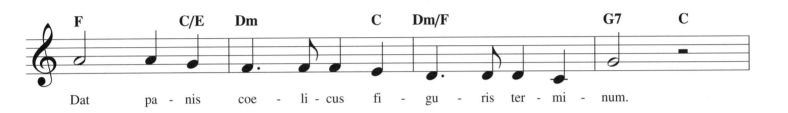

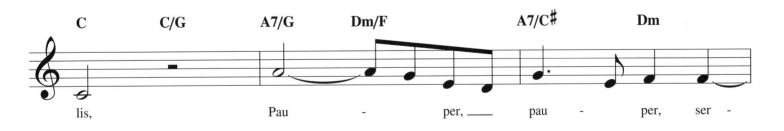

HE IS AN ENGLISHMAN
from *HMS Pinafore*

ARTHUR SULLIVAN
W.S. GILBERT

TIT-WILLOW
from *The Mikado*

ARTHUR SULLIVAN
W.S. GILBERT

LITTLE BUTTERCUP
from *HMS Pinafore*

ARTHUR SULLIVAN
W.S. GILBERT

Moderate Waltz tempo

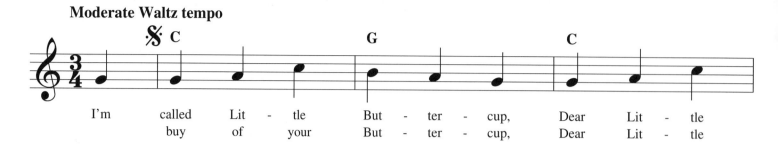

I'm called Lit - tle But - ter - cup, Dear Lit - tle
buy of your But - ter - cup, Dear Lit - tle

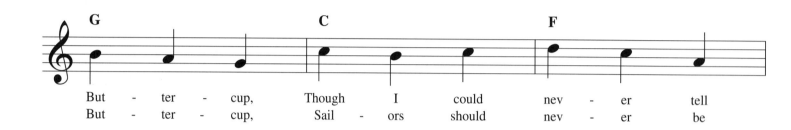

But - ter - cup, Though I could nev - er tell
But - ter - cup, Sail - ors should nev - er be

why; But still I'm called But - ter - cup,
shy; So buy of your But - ter - cup,

Poor Lit - tle But - ter - cup, Sweet Lit - tle But - ter - cup,

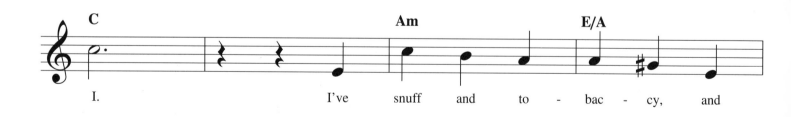

I. I've snuff and to - bac - cy, and

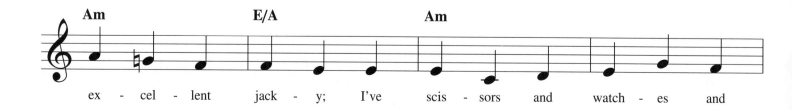

ex - cel - lent jack - y; I've scis - sors and watch - es and

WE SAIL THE OCEAN BLUE
from *HMS Pinafore*

ARTHUR SULLIVAN
W.S. GILBERT

Allegretto pesante

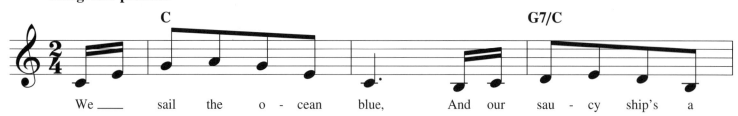

We __ sail the o - cean blue, And our sau - cy ship's a

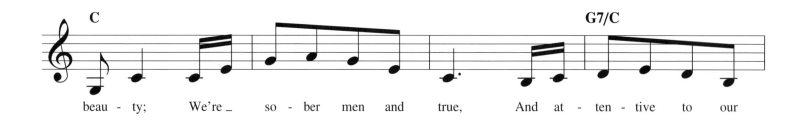

beau - ty; We're _ so - ber men and true, And at - ten - tive to our

du - ty. When the balls whis - tle free O'er the bright __ blue sea, We

stand to our guns all day; __ When at an - chor we ride On the

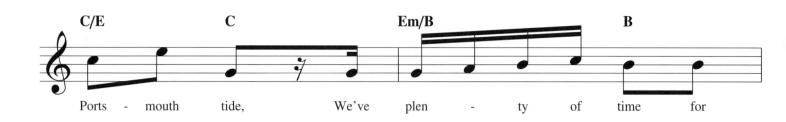

Ports - mouth tide, We've plen - ty of time for

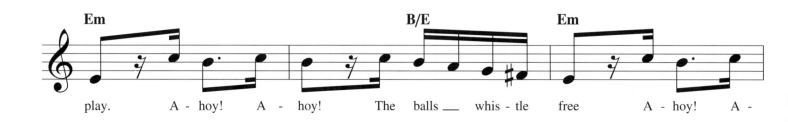

play. A - hoy! A - hoy! The balls __ whis - tle free A - hoy! A -

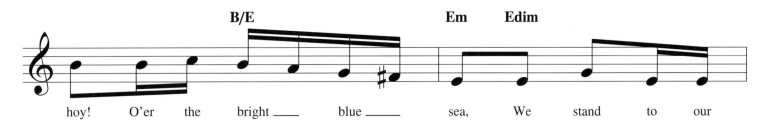

hoy! O'er the bright ___ blue ___ sea, We stand to our

guns, to our guns all day. _____ We ___ sail the o - cean

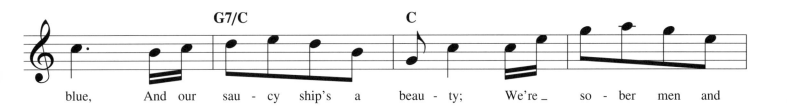

blue, And our sau - cy ship's a beau - ty; We're _ so - ber men and

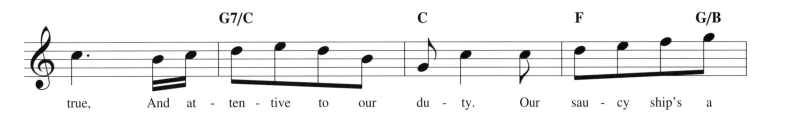

true, And at - ten - tive to our du - ty. Our sau - cy ship's a

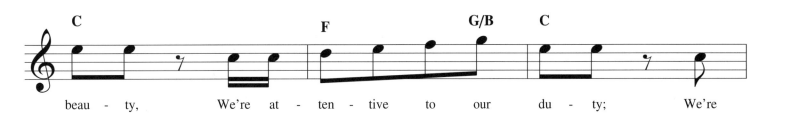

beau - ty, We're at - ten - tive to our du - ty; We're

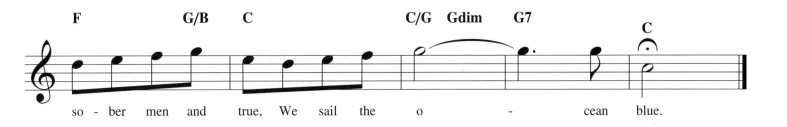

so - ber men and true, We sail the o - cean blue.

CARO MIO BEN

GIUSEPPE GIORDANI

Larghetto

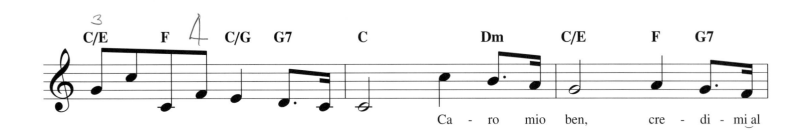

Ca - ro mio ben, cre - di - mi al

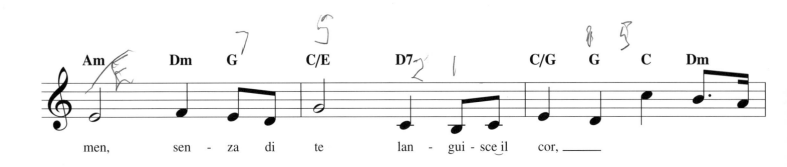

men, sen - za di te lan - gui - sce il cor, _____

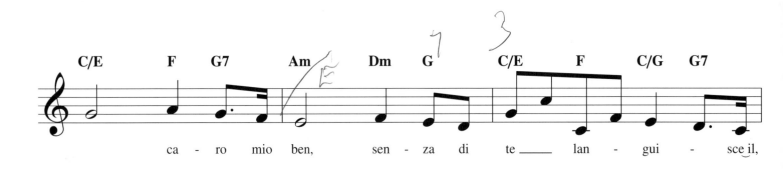

ca - ro mio ben, sen - za di te _____ lan - gui - sce il,

cor.   Il tuo fe -

75

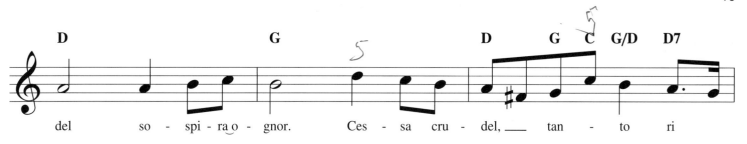

del so - spi - ra o - gnor. Ces - sa cru - del, ___ tan - to ri

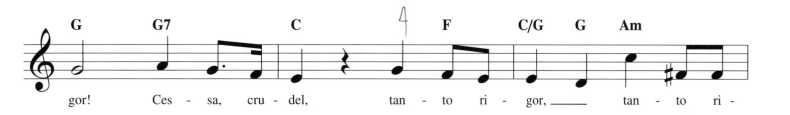

gor! Ces - sa, cru - del, tan - to ri - gor, ___ tan - to ri -

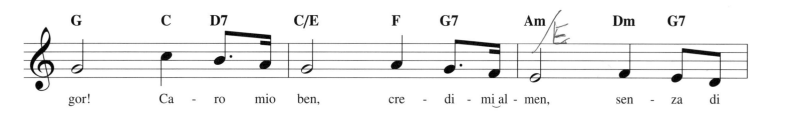

gor! Ca - ro mio ben, cre - di - mi al - men, sen - za di

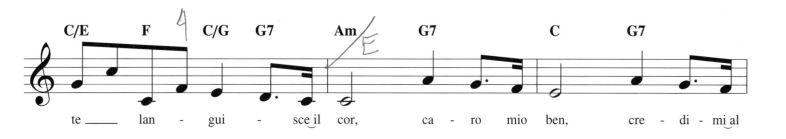

te ___ lan - gui - sce il cor, ca - ro mio ben, cre - di - mi al

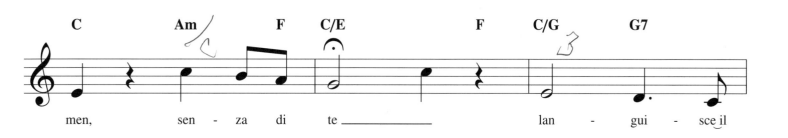

men, sen - za di te ___ lan - gui - sce il

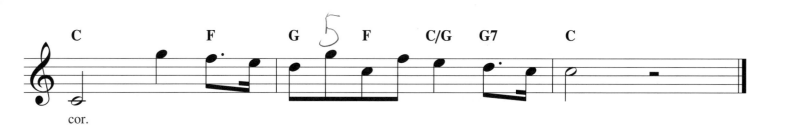

cor.

CHE FARÒ SENZA EURIDICE

from *Orfeo ed Euridice*

CHRISTOPH WILLIBALD VON GLUCK

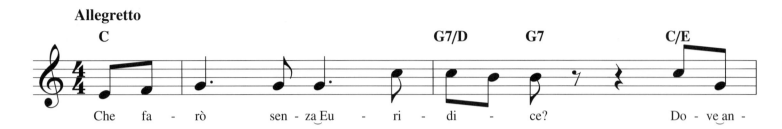

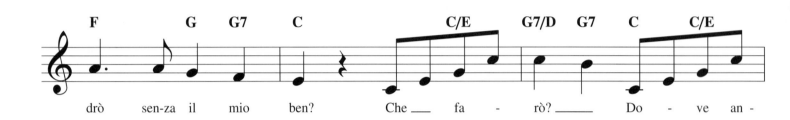

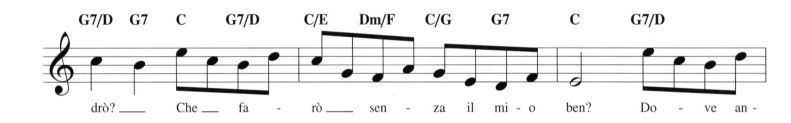

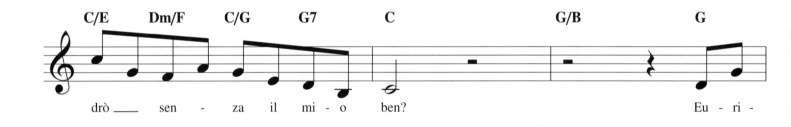

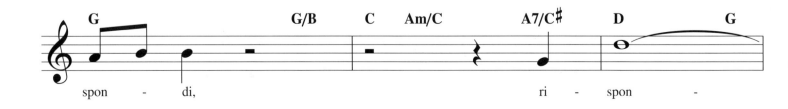

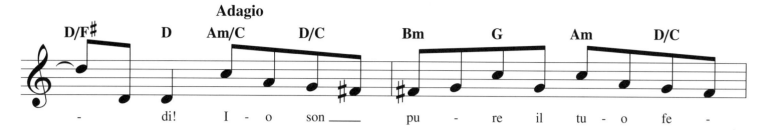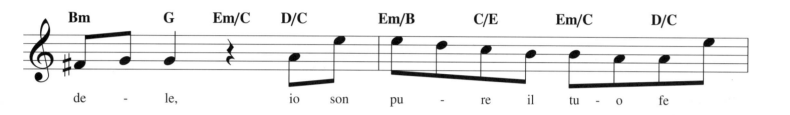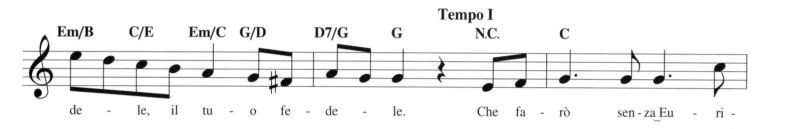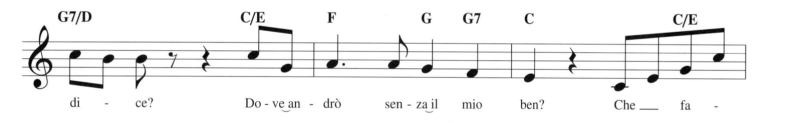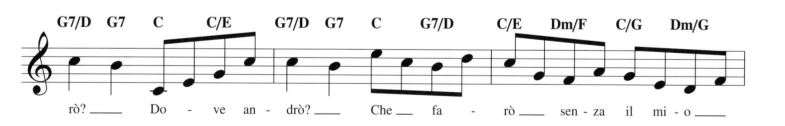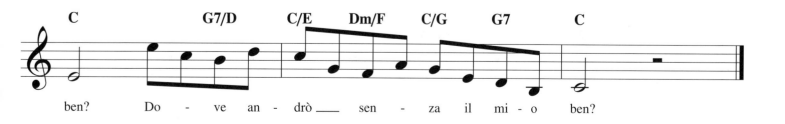

BERCEUSE
from *Jocelyn*

BENJAMIN GODARD`

GAVOTTE

FRANÇOIS GOSSEC

AVE MARIA

CHARLES GOUNOD

Reverently

A - ve, Ma - ri - a!

Gra - ti - a ple - na. Do - mi - nus

Te - cum be - ne - dic - ta

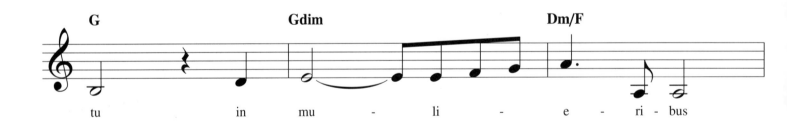

tu in mu - li - e - ri - bus

et _____ be - ne - dic - tus fruc - tus _____

ven - tris _____ tu - i Je - sus.

Sanc - ta ____ Ma - ri - a. Sanc - ta ____ Ma - ri - a ____ Ma -

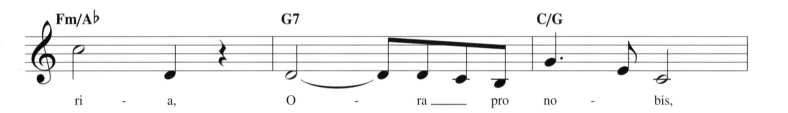

ri - a, O - ra ____ pro no - bis,

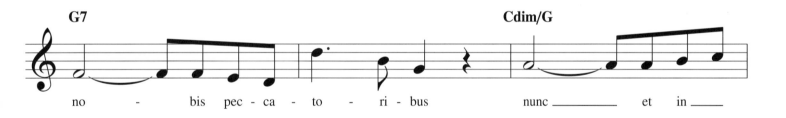

no - bis pec - ca - to - ri - bus nunc _____ et in ____

Ho - ra, in ho - ra ____ mor - tis ____ nos - trae. ____

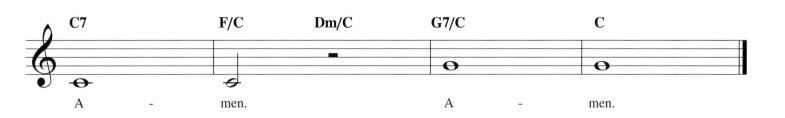

A - men. A - men.

ENTREAT ME NOT TO LEAVE THEE
(Song of Ruth)

CHARLES GOUNOD

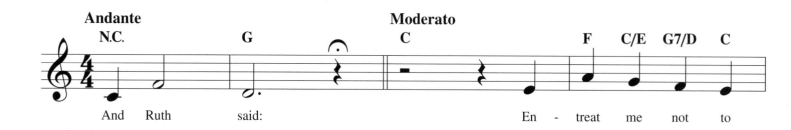

And Ruth said: En-treat me not to

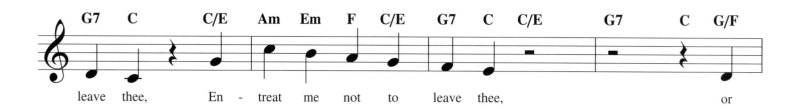

leave thee, En-treat me not to leave thee, or

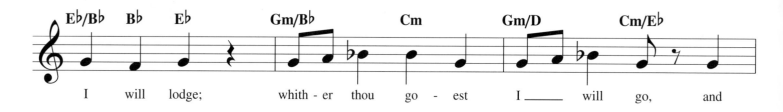

to re-turn from fol-low-ing af-ter thee, for

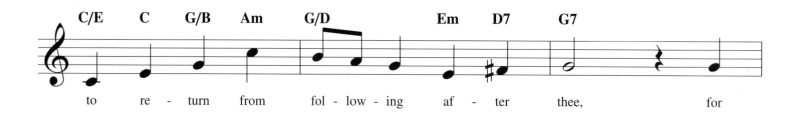

whith-er thou go-est I will go, and where thou lodg-est

I will lodge; whith-er thou go-est I ___ will go, and

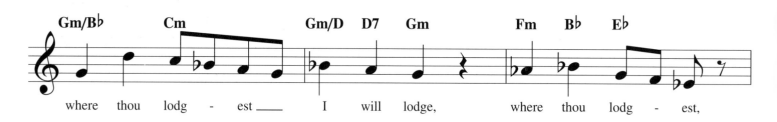

where thou lodg-est ___ I will lodge, where thou lodg-est,

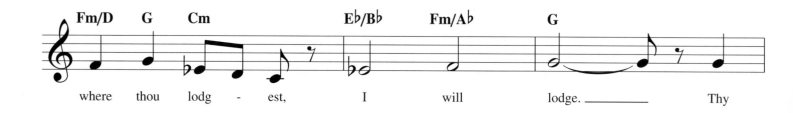

where thou lodg-est, I will lodge. ___ Thy

peo - ple shall be my peo - ple, and thy ___ God, my

God, ___ thy peo - ple shall be my peo - ple, and thy

God, ___ my God; ___ Thy peo - ple shall be my peo - ple, and thy

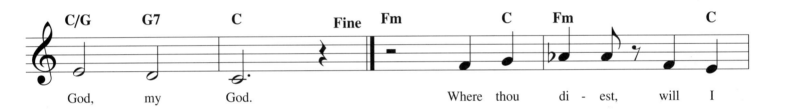

God, my God. Where thou di - est, will I

die, ___ and there will I be bur - ied; ___ The Lord do

so to me, and more al - so, if aught but death part thee and

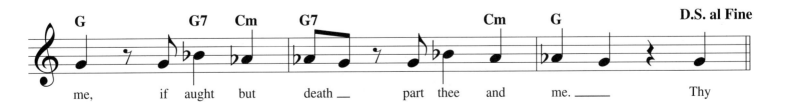

me, if aught but death ___ part thee and me. ___ Thy

FUNERAL MARCH OF A MARIONETTE

CHARLES GOUNOD

Allegretto

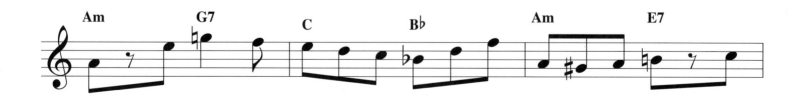

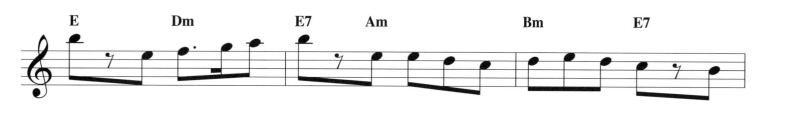

O DIVINE REDEEMER

CHARLES GOUNOD

Molto moderato

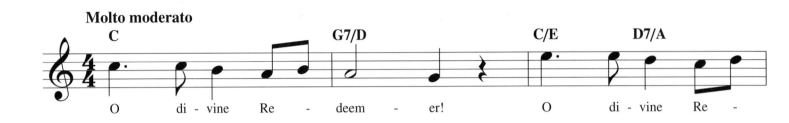

O di - vine Re - deem - er! O di - vine Re -

deem - er! I pray Thee, grant __ me __ par - don, __ and re -

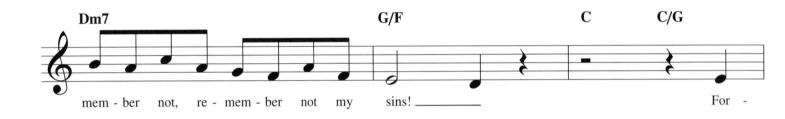

mem - ber not, re - mem - ber not my sins! __ For -

give me, O di - vine Re - deem - er! I

pray Thee, grant __ me __ par - don, __ and re - mem - ber not, re - mem - ber not, O

Lord, my sins! Night gath - ers round my

soul; _____ fear - ful, I cry to Thee; _____

Come to mine aid, O Lord! _____ Haste Thee, Lord, haste to

help me! Hear my cry, _____ hear my cry! _____

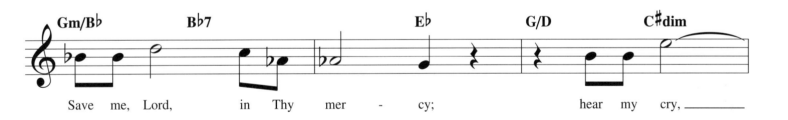

Save me, Lord, in Thy mer - cy; hear my cry, _____

_____ hear my cry! Come and save me, O Lord! _____

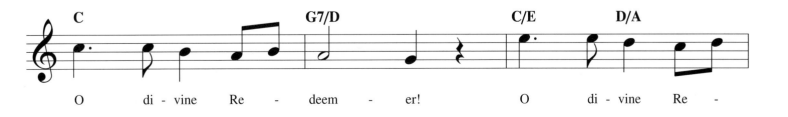

O di - vine Re - deem - er! O di - vine Re -

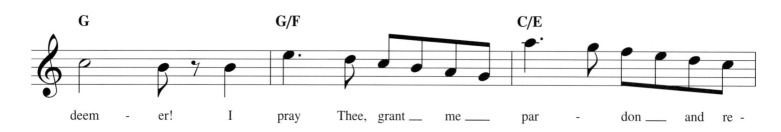

deem - er! I pray Thee, grant ___ me ___ par - don ___ and re -

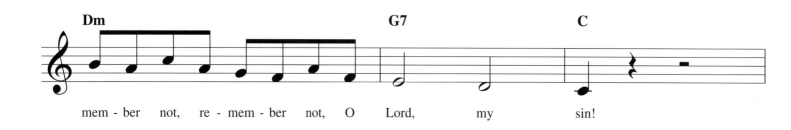

mem - ber not, re - mem - ber not, O Lord, my sin!

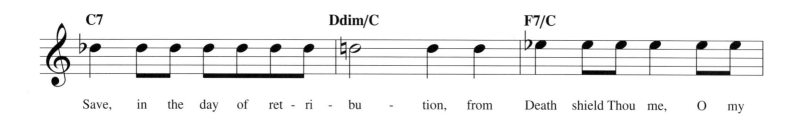

Save, in the day of ret - ri - bu - tion, from Death shield Thou me, O my

God! O di - vine Re - deem - er, have

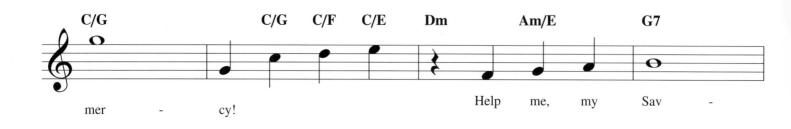

mer - cy! Help me, my Sav -

ior!

AIR
from *Water Music*

GEORGE FRIDERIC HANDEL

Andante

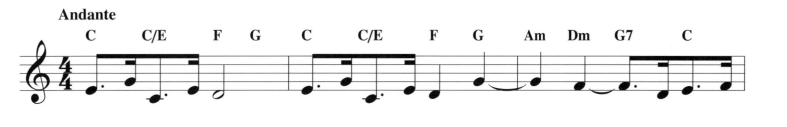

THE HARMONIOUS BLACKSMITH

GEORGE FRIDERIC HANDEL

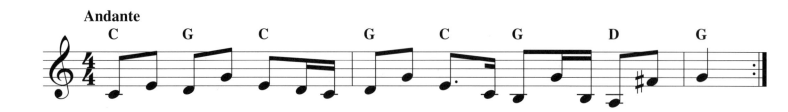

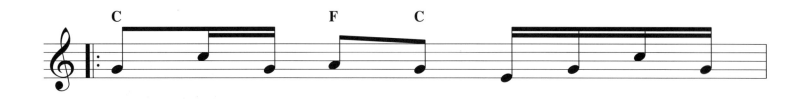

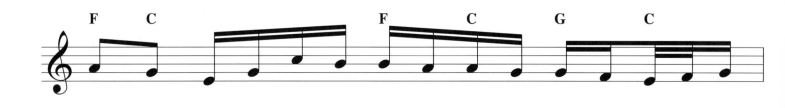

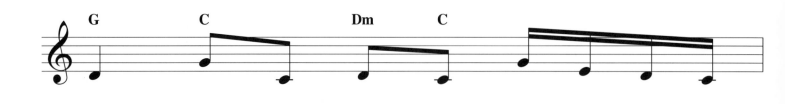

HORNPIPE
from *Water Music*

George Frideric Handel

LARGO
from *Xerxes*

GEORGE FRIDERIC HANDEL

Larghetto

Om - bra ma - i

fù   (Instrumental)   di ve - ge -

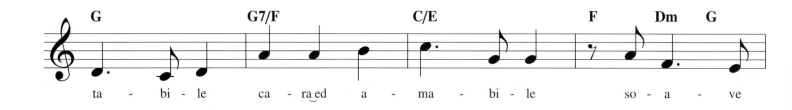

ta - bi - le ca - ra ed a - ma - bi - le so - a - ve

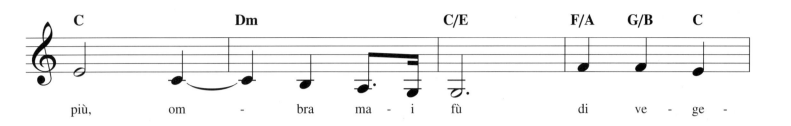

più, om - bra ma - i fù di ve - ge -

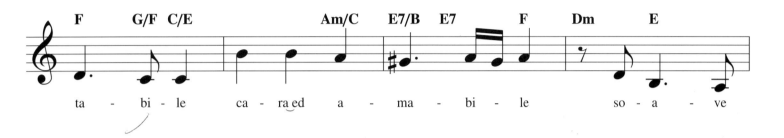

ta - bi - le ca - ra ed a - ma - bi - le so - a - ve

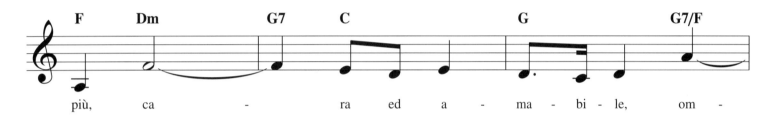

più, ca - ra ed a - ma - bi - le, om -

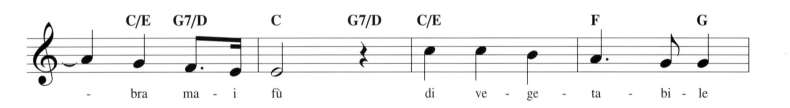

- bra ma - i fù di ve - ge - ta - bi - le

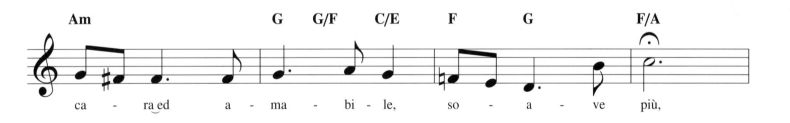

ca - ra ed a - ma - bi - le, so - a - ve più,

so - a - ve più.

PASTORAL SYMPHONY
from *Messiah*

GEORGE FRIDERIC HANDEL

Larghetto

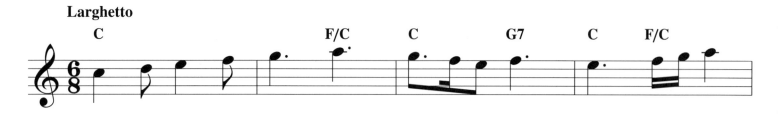

ST. ANTHONY CHORALE

FRANZ JOSEPH HAYDN

SYMPHONY NO. 94 ("SURPRISE")
Second Movement Theme

FRANZ JOSEPH HAYDN

TOYLAND
from *Babes in Toyland*

VICTOR HERBERT

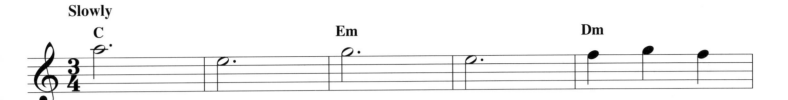

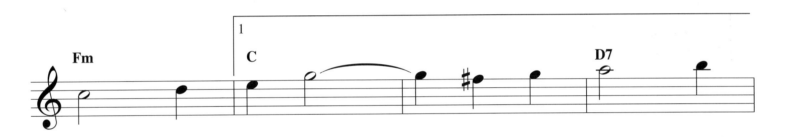

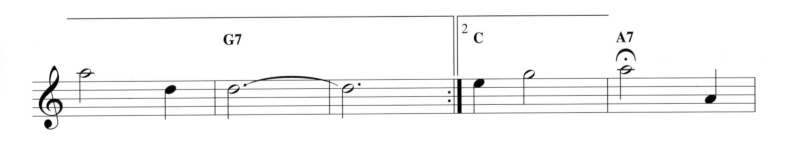

ICH LIEBE DICH
(I Love You)

EDVARD GRIEG

Moderately slow

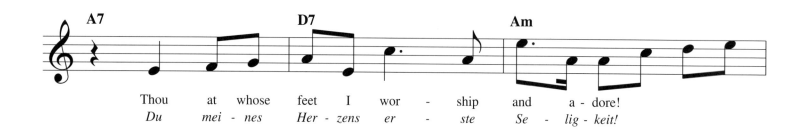

Light of my life whose im - age my heart hold - eth!
Du mein Ge - dan ke, du mein Sein und Wer - den!

Thou at whose feet I wor - ship and a - dore!
Du mei - nes Her - zens er - ste Se - lig - keit!

With wings of love my spir - it thee en -
Ich lie - be dich wie nichts auf die - ser

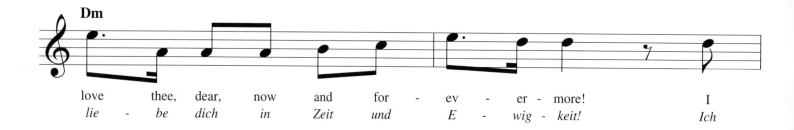

fold - eth, I love thee, dear, I love thee, dear, I
Er - den, ich lie - be dich, ich lie - be dich, ich

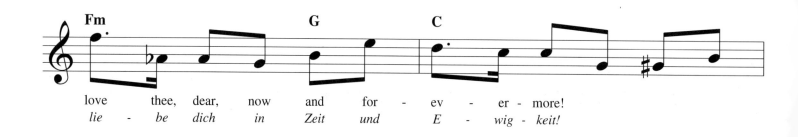

love thee, dear, now and for - ev - er - more! I
lie - be dich in Zeit und E - wig - keit! Ich

love thee, dear, now and for - ev - er - more!
lie - be dich in Zeit und E - wig - keit!

I think of
Ich den - ke

thee in dream - ing and in wak - ing, Thy per - fect
dein, kann stets nur dei - ne den - ken, nur dei - nem

bliss I set all else be - fore;
Glück ist die - ses Herzge - weiht;

Wher - ev - er fate my foot - steps may be tak - ing, I
wie Gott auch mag des Le - bens Schick - sal len - ken ich

love thee, dear, I love thee, dear, I love thee, dear, now and for -
lie - be dich, ich lie - be dich, ich lie - be dich in Zeit und

ev - er - more. I love thee, dear, now and for - ev - er - more!
E - wig - keit! Ich lie - be dich in Zeit und E - wig - keit!

IN THE HALL OF THE MOUNTAIN KING

from *Peer Gynt*

EDVARD GRIEG

Alla marcia e molto marcato

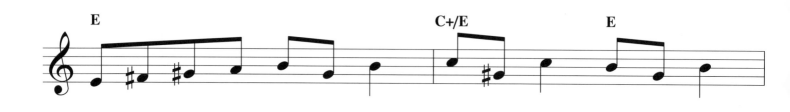

MORNING
from *Peer Gynt*

EDVARD GRIEG

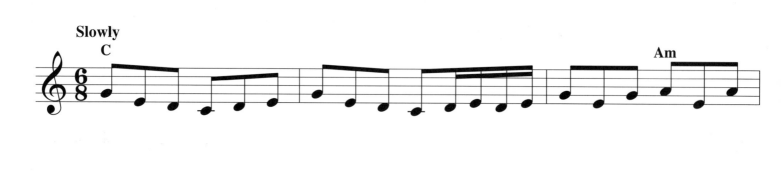

SOLVEJG'S SONG
from *Peer Gynt*

EDVARD GRIEG

EVENING PRAYER
from *Hansel and Gretel*

ENGELBERT HUMPERDINCK

Moderato

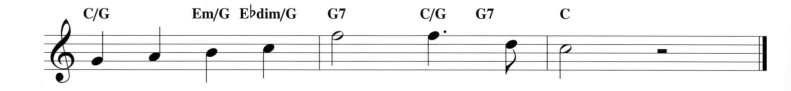

MEDITATION
from *Thaïs*

JULES MASSENET

Andante religioso

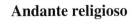

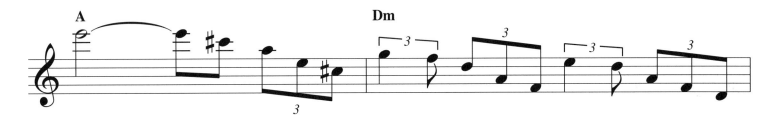

MATTINATA

RUGGERO LEONCAVALLO

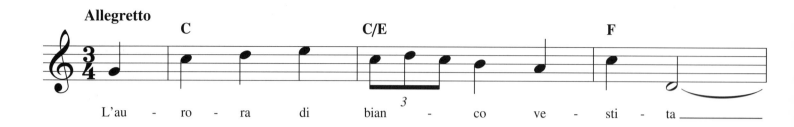

L'au - ro - ra di bian - co ve - sti - ta _____

____ Giá l'us - cio dis - chiu - de al gran

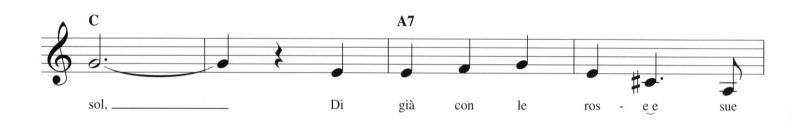

sol, _____ Di già con le ros - e e sue

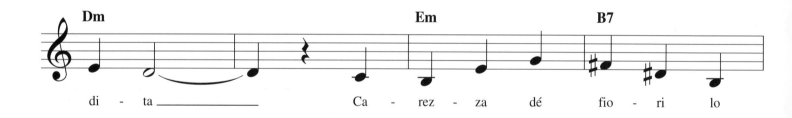

di - ta _____ Ca - rez - za dé fio - ri lo

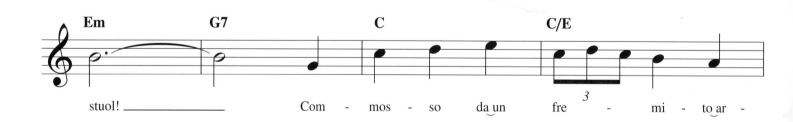

stuol! _____ Com - mos - so da un fre - mi - to ar -

ca - no _____ In - tor - noil

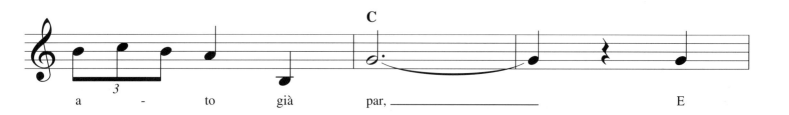

a - to già par, _____ E

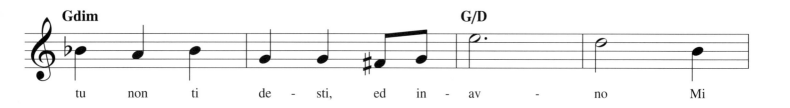

tu non ti de - sti, ed in - av - no Mi

sto qui do - len - te a can - tar. _____

Met - ti an - che tu la ve - ste bian - ca

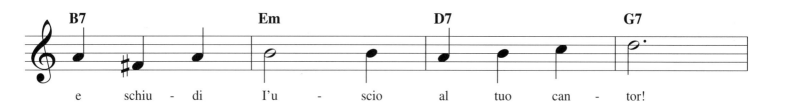

e schiu - di l'u - scio al tuo can - tor!

O - ve non se - i la lu - ce man - ca,

O - ve tu se - i nas - ce l'a - mor!

TO A WILD ROSE
from *Woodland Sketches*

EDWARD MACDOWELL

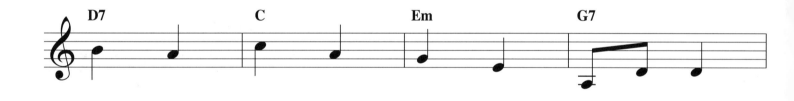

WEDDING MARCH
from *A Midsummer Night's Dream*

FELIX MENDELSSOHN

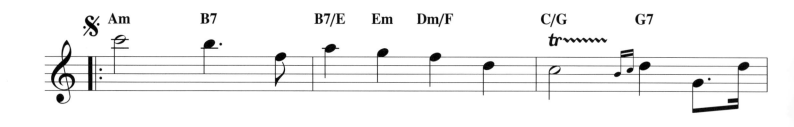

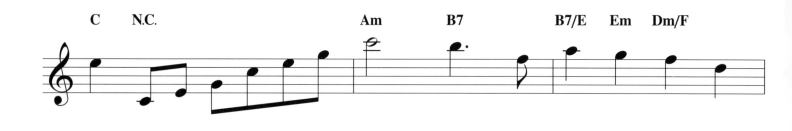

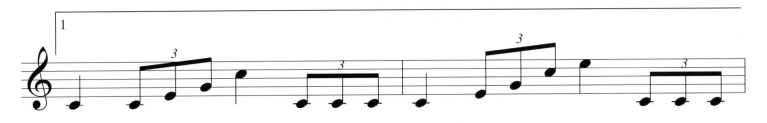

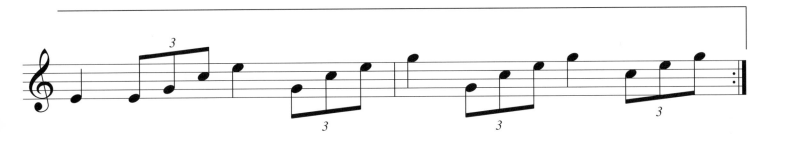

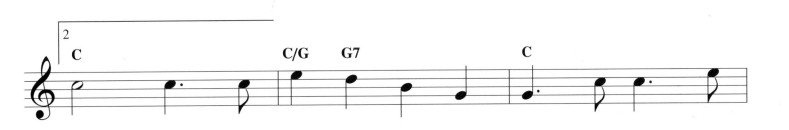

D.S. al Fine

SPRING SONG
from *Songs Without Words*

FELIX MENDELSSOHN

RONDEAU

JEAN-JOSEPH MOURET

ALLELUIA
from *Exsultate, jubilate*

WOLFGANG AMADEUS MOZART

Allegro non troppo

Al - le - lu - ia, al - le - lu - ia, _____

al - le - lu - ia, al - le - lu - ia,

al - le - lu - ia, al - le - lu - ia, _____

al - le - lu - ia, al - le - lu - ia.

Al - le - lu - ia, al - le - lu - ia,

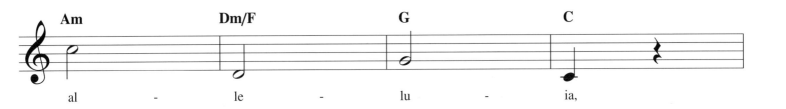

al - le - lu - ia,

al - le - lu - ia, al - le - lu - ia,

al - le - lu - ia, al -

le - lu - ia.

EINE KLEINE NACHTMUSIK
First Movement Theme

WOLFGANG AMADEUS MOZART

EINE KLEINE NACHTMUSIK
Second Movement Theme ("Romanze")

WOLFGANG AMADEUS MOZART

EINE KLEINE NACHTMUSIK
Fourth Movement Theme

WOLFGANG AMADEUS MOZART

GERMAN DANCE

WOLFGANG AMADEUS MOZART

Stately

MINUET
from *Don Giovanni*

WOLFGANG AMADEUS MOZART

Stately

MINUET, K 2

WOLFGANG AMADEUS MOZART

PAPAGENO'S SONG
from *The Magic Flute*

WOLFGANG AMADEUS MOZART

TURKISH RONDO
(Rondo Alla Turca)
from *Sonata K 331, Third Movement*

WOLFGANG AMADEUS MOZART

THE GREAT GATE OF KIEV
from *Pictures at an Exhibition*

MODEST MUSSORGSKY

Allegro alla breve, maestoso con grandezza

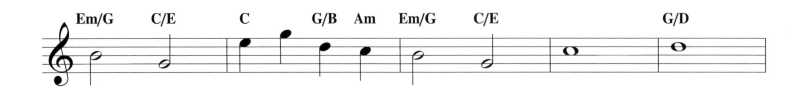

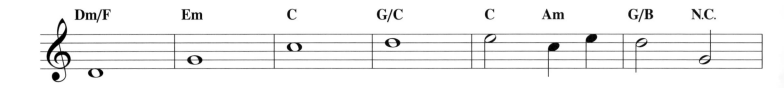

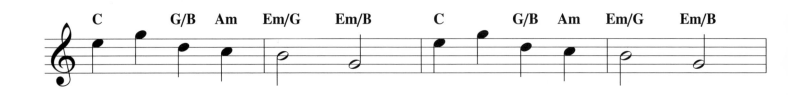

CAN CAN
from *Orpheus in the Underworld*

JACQUES O

Allegro

BARCAROLLE
from *The Tales of Hoffmann*

JACQUES OFFENBACH

Moderato

Bel - le nuit, ô nuit ___ d'a-mour, Sou - ris ___ à nos i - vres - ses.

Nuit plus dou - ce que ___ le jour, Ô bel - le nuit d'a - mour!

Le temps fuit et sans re - tour. Em - por - te nos ten - dres - ses!

Loin de cet heu - reux sè - jour, Le temps fuit sans re - tour. ___ Zé -

phirs ___ em - bra - sés, ___ Ver - sez - nous vos ca - res - ses, Zé -

phirs ___ em - bra - sés, ___ Don - nez - nous vos bai - sers,

vos ___ bai - sers, vos ___ bai - sers. Ah! ___

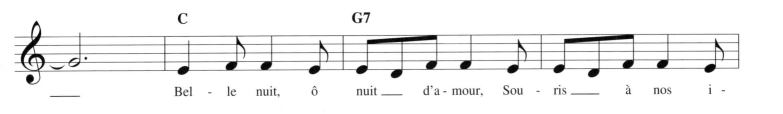

Bel - le nuit, ô nuit __ d'a-mour, Sou - ris __ à nos i -

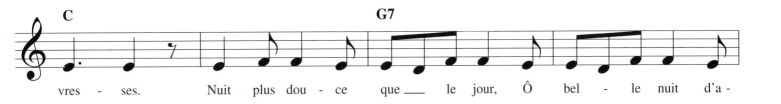

vres - ses. Nuit plus dou - ce que __ le jour, Ô bel - le nuit d'a -

mour! Ô bel - le nuit d'a - mour! Ah! Sou - ris à nos i -

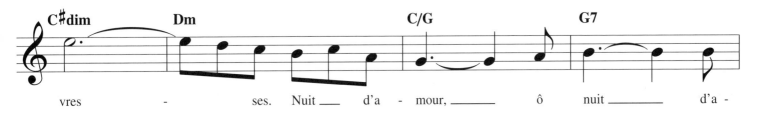

vres - ses. Nuit __ d'a - mour, __ ô nuit __ d'a -

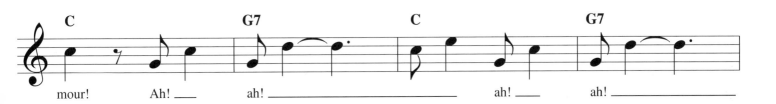

mour! Ah! __ ah! __ ah! __ ah! __

__ ah! __ ah! __ ah! __

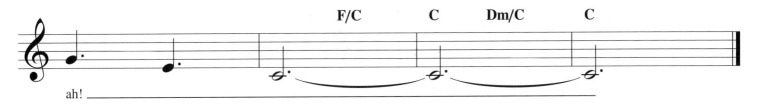

ah! __

CANON

JOHANN PACHELBEL

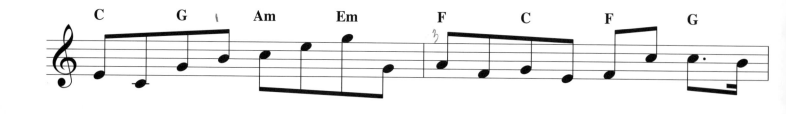

O MIO BABBINO CARO

from *Gianni Schicchi*

GIACOMO PUCCINI

Andantino ingenuo

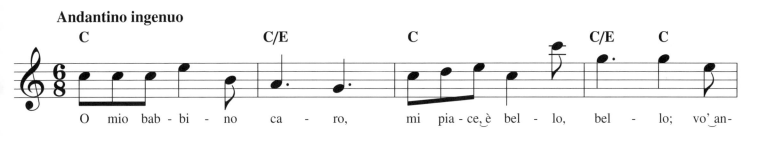

O mio bab-bi - no ca - ro, mi pia-ce,è bel - lo, bel - lo; vo' an-

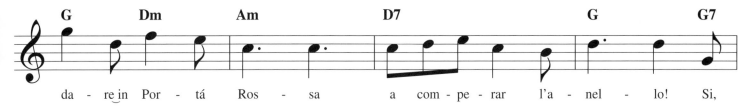

da - re in Por - tá Ros - sa a com-pe-rar l'a - nel - lo! Si,

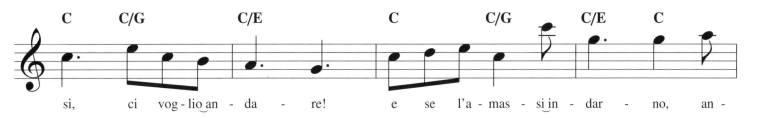

si, ci vog-lio an-da - re! e se l'a - mas-si in - dar - no, an -

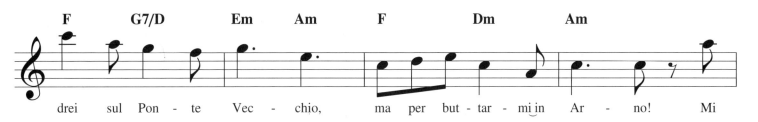

drei sul Pon - te Vec - chio, ma per but-tar - mi in Ar - no! Mi

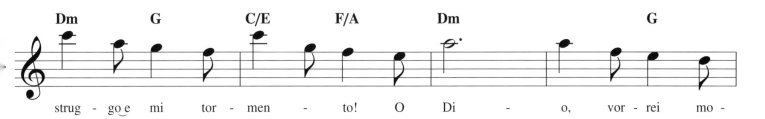

strug - go e mi tor - men - to! O Di - o, vor-rei mo-

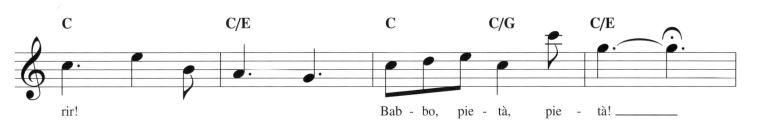

rir!   Bab - bo, pie - tà, pie - tà! _____

bab - bo, pie - tà, pie - tà!...

QUANDO MEN VO
("Musetta's Waltz")
from *La Bohème*

GIACOMO PUCCINI

Tempo di Valse lento

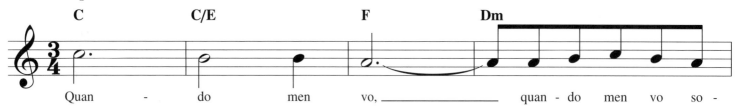

Quan - do men vo, _____ quan - do men vo so -

let - ta per la via la gen - te so sta e mi - ra.

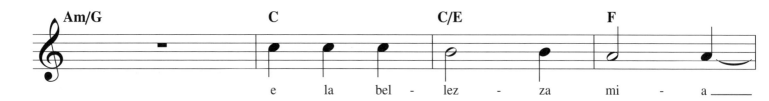

e la bel - lez - za mi - a _____

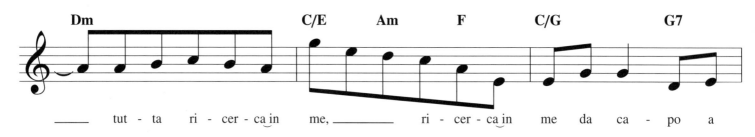

_____ tut - ta ri - cer - ca in me, _____ ri - cer - ca in me da ca - po a

piè. Ed as - sa -

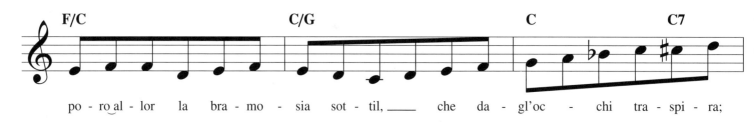

po - ro al - lor la bra - mo - sia sot - til, ____ che da - gl'oc - chi tra - spi - ra;

e dai pa - le - si vez - zi in - ten - der sa _____ al - le oc -

MINUET

IGNACY JAN PADEREWSKI

With expression

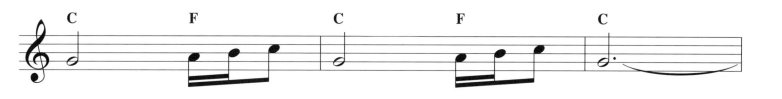

RONDEAU
from *Abdelazer*

HENRY PURCELL

Con brio

TRUMPET TUNE

Henry Purcell

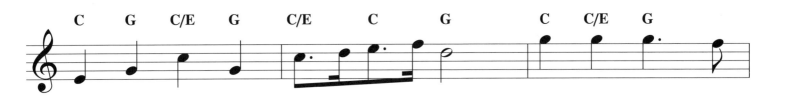

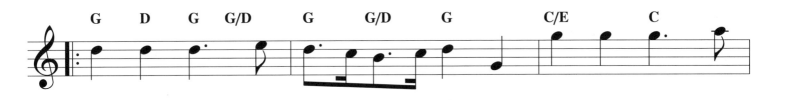

SONG OF INDIA

NIKOLAY RIMSKY-KORSAKOV

LA CUMPARSITA

G. RODRIGUEZ

Moderato

OVER THE WAVES
(Excerpt)

JUVENTINO ROSAS

Waltz tempo

MELODY

ANTON RUBINSTEIN

AVE MARIA

FRANZ SCHUBERT

Sehr langsam (Molto adagio)

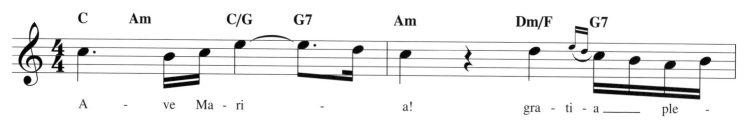

A - ve Ma - ri - a! gra - ti - a _____ ple -

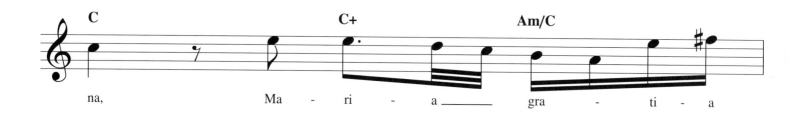

na, Ma - ri - a _____ gra - ti - a

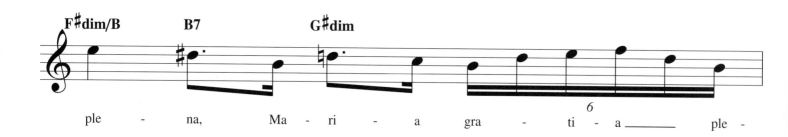

ple - na, Ma - ri - a gra - ti - a _____ ple -

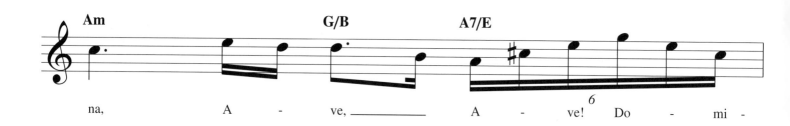

na, A - ve, _____ A - ve! Do - mi -

nus, Do - mi - nus _____ te - cum, Be - ne -

dic - ta tu in mu - li - e - ri - bus, et

be - ne - dic - tus, et

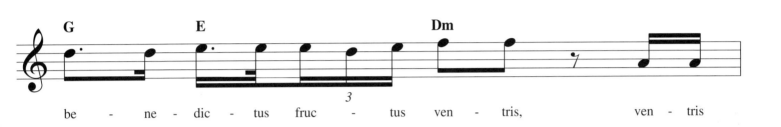

be - ne - dic - tus fruc - tus ven - tris, ven - tris

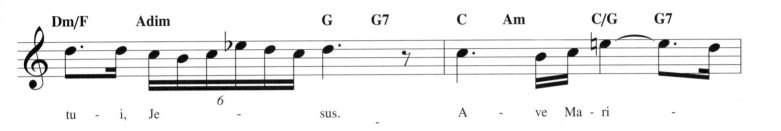

tu - i, Je - sus. A - ve Ma - ri -

a!

SERENADE
from *Schwanengesang*

FRANZ SCHUBERT

Slowly

Lei - se fle - hen mei - ne Lie - der durch die Nacht _ zu
Hörst die Nach - ti - gal - len schla - gen? Ach! sie fle - hen

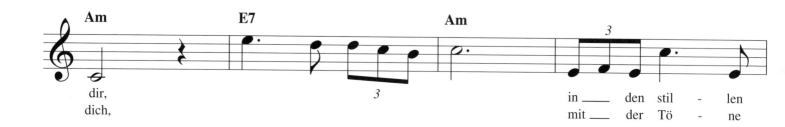

dir,
dich,

in ___ den stil - len
mit ___ der Tö - ne

Hain _ her - nie - der, Leib - chen, komm _ zu mir.
sü - ßen Kla - gen fle - hen sie ___ für mich.

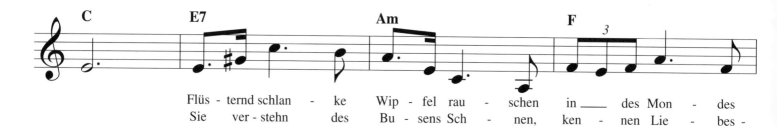

Flüs - ternd schlan - ke Wip - fel rau - schen in ___ des Mon - des
Sie ver - stehn des Bu - sens Seh - nen, ken - nen Lie - bes-

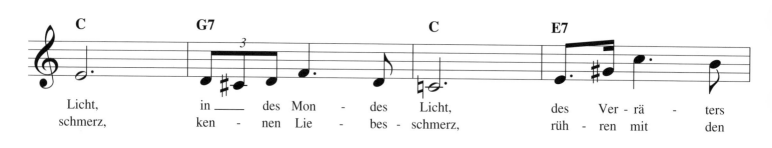

Licht, in ___ des Mon - des Licht, des Ver - rä - ters
schmerz, ken - nen Lie - bes - schmerz, rüh - ren mit den

feind - lich Lau - schen fürch - te, Hol - de, nicht, fürch - te, Hol - de,
Sil - ber - tö - nen je - des wei - che Herz, je - des wei - che

ABOUT STRANGE LANDS AND PEOPLE

from *Scenes from Childhood*

ROBERT SCHUMANN

Moderato

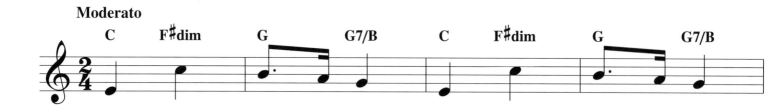

THE HAPPY FARMER
from *Album for the Young*

ROBERT SCHUMANN

Allegro animato

REVERIE
from *Scenes from Childhood*

ROBERT SCHUMANN

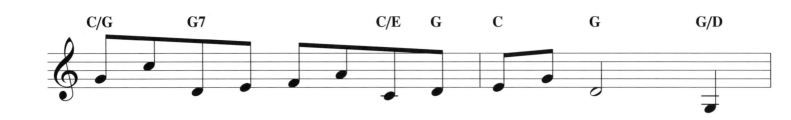

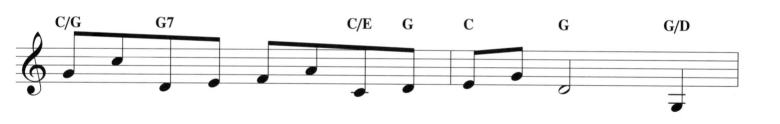

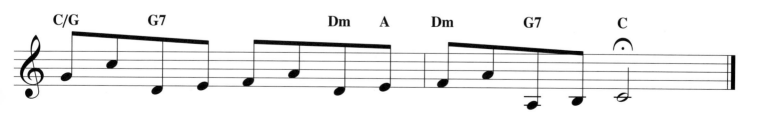

THE MOLDAU
(Excerpt)
from *Má Vlast*

BEDRICH SMETANA

SEMPER FIDELIS

JOHN PHILIP SOUSA

March tempo

THE LIBERTY BELL MARCH

JOHN PHILIP SOUSA

March tempo, in 2

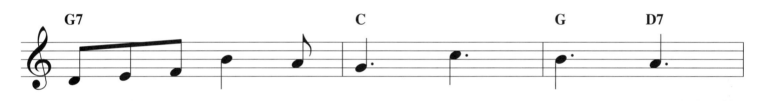

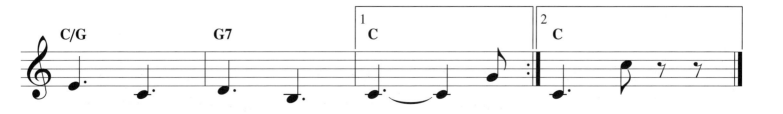

THE STARS AND STRIPES FOREVER
(Excerpt)

JOHN PHILIP SOUSA

March tempo

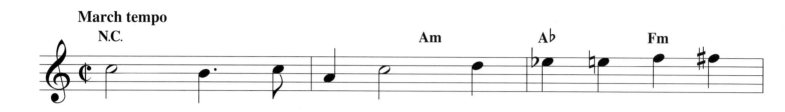

THE WASHINGTON POST MARCH

JOHN PHILIP SOUSA

163

BIST DU BEI MIR

G.H. STÖZEL
(formerly attributed to J.S. Bach)

Gently (not too slow)

Bist du bei mir, geh' ich mit Freu - den

zum Ster - ben ___ und zu mei - ner ___ Ruh', zum ___

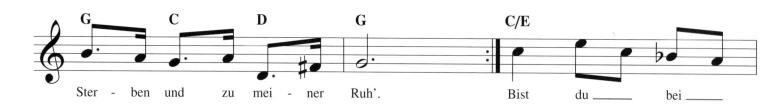

Ster - ben und zu mei - ner Ruh'. Bist du ___ bei ___

mir, geh' ich mit Freu - den zum Ster - ben ___

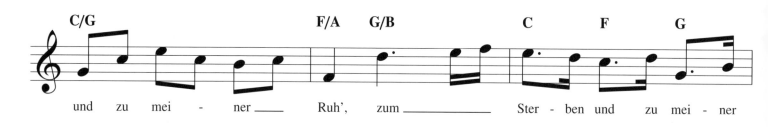

und zu mei - ner ___ Ruh', zum ___ Ster - ben und zu mei - ner

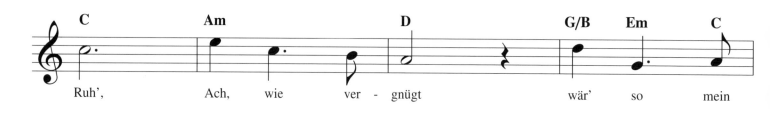

Ruh', Ach, wie ver - gnügt wär' so mein

En - de, es drück - ten ___ dei - ne schö - nen ___

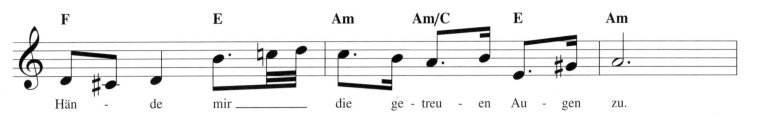

Hän - de mir _____ die ge - treu - en Au - gen zu.

Ach, wie ver - gnügt wär' so mein

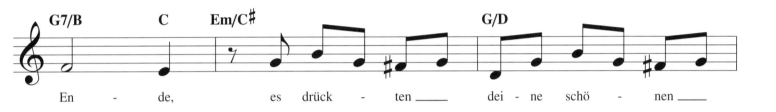

En - de, es drück - ten _____ dei - ne schö - nen _____

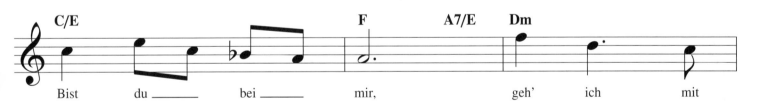

Hän - de mir _____ die ge - treu - en Au - gen zu.

Bist du _____ bei _____ mir, geh' ich mit

Freu - den zum Ster - ben _____ und zu mei - ner _____

Ruh', zum _____ Ster - ben und zu mei - ner Ruh'.

EMPEROR WALTZ
(Excerpt)

JOHANN STRAUSS, JR.

ON THE BEAUTIFUL BLUE DANUBE
(Excerpt)

JOHANN STRAUSS, JR.

ROSES FROM THE SOUTH
(Excerpt)

JOHANN STRAUSS, JR.

Waltz tempo

TALES FROM THE VIENNA WOODS
(Excerpt)

JOHANN STRAUSS, JR.

Waltz tempo

VIENNA LIFE
(Excerpt)

JOHANN STRAUSS, JR.

Waltz tempo

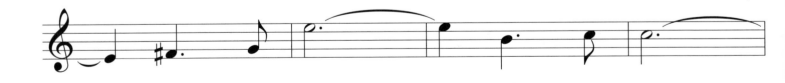

PIZZICATO POLKA

JOHANN and JOSEF STRAUSS

Bright Polka tempo

**D.S. al Fine
(with repeat)**

HEARTS AND FLOWERS

THEODORE M. TOBANI

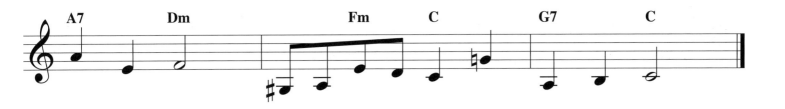

1812 OVERTURE
(Excerpt)

PYOTR IL'YICH TCHAIKOVSKY

SLEEPING BEAUTY WALTZ

PYOTR IL'YICH TCHAIKOVSKY

SWAN LAKE THEME

PYOTR IL'YICH TCHAIK

WALTZ
from *Swan Lake*

PYOTR IL'YICH TCHAIKOVSKY

Tempo di valse

VIVE L'AMOUR

Traditional European

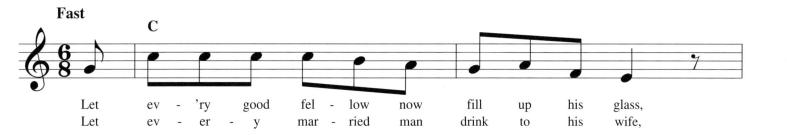

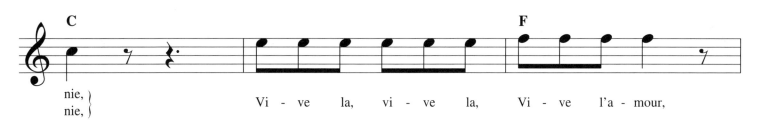

SERENATA

ENRICO TOSELLI

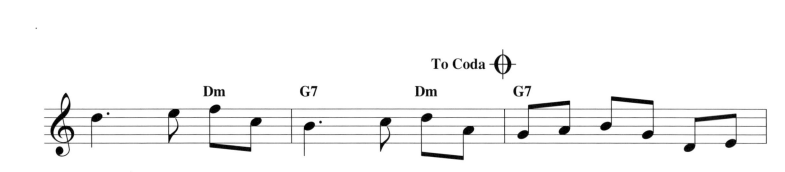

LA DONNA È MOBILE
from *Rigoletto*

GIUSEPPE VERDI

TRIUMPHAL MARCH
from *Aïda*

GIUSEPPE VERDI

Stately

LIBIAMO
("Drinking Song")
from *La Traviata*

GIUSEPPE VERDI

Allegretto

Li - bia - mo, li - bia - mo ne'

lie - ti ca - li - ci, che la ___ bel -

lez - za ___ in - fio - ra; e la ___

___ fug - ge - vol, fug - ge - vol o -

- ra s'in ne - brii ___ a ___ vo - lut -

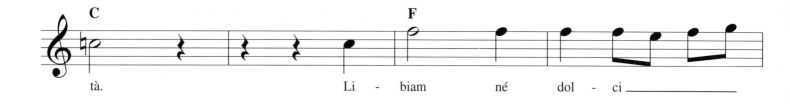

tà. Li - biam né dol - ci ___

fre - mi - ti che su - sci - ta l'a -

mo - re, poi - chè quel - l'oc - chio __ al __

co - re on - ni - po - ten - te ___

va. ___ Li - bia - mo, a -

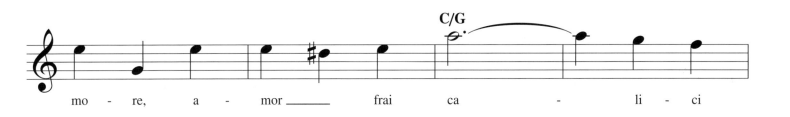

mo - re, a - mor ___ frai ca - li - ci

più cal - di ___ ba - ci ___ a - vra. ___

189

BRIDAL CHORUS
from *Lohengrin*

RICHARD WAGNER

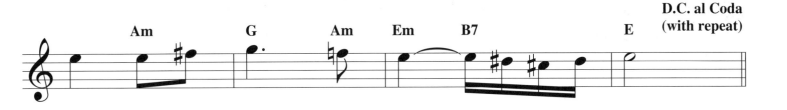

PILGRIMS' CHORUS

from *Tannhäuser*

RICHARD WAGNER

Andante maestoso

ANGEL OF LOVE

EMIL WALDTEUFEL

Waltz tempo

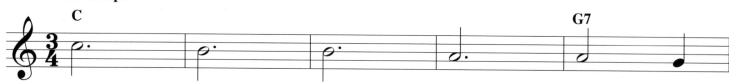

THE SKATERS
(Waltz)

EMIL WALDTEUFEL

Moderate Waltz

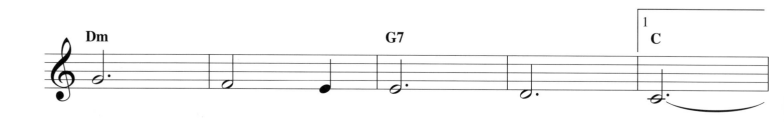

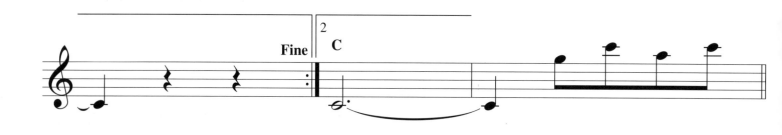

LA PALOMA

SEBASTIAN YRADIER

CHORD SPELLER

C chords

C	C–E–G
Cm	C–E♭–G
C7	C–E–G–B♭
Cdim	C–E♭–G♭
C+	C–E–G♯

C♯ or D♭ chords

C♯	C♯–F–G♯
C♯m	C♯–E–G♯
C♯7	C♯–F–G♯–B
C♯dim	C♯–E–G
C♯+	C♯–F–A

D chords

D	D–F♯–A
Dm	D–F–A
D7	D–F♯–A–C
Ddim	D–F–A♭
D+	D–F♯–A♯

E♭ chords

E♭	E♭–G–B♭
E♭m	E♭–G♭–B♭
E♭7	E♭–G–B♭–D♭
E♭dim	E♭–G♭–A
E♭+	E♭–G–B

E chords

E	E–G♯–B
Em	E–G–B
E7	E–G♯–B–D
Edim	E–G–B♭
E+	E–G♯–C

F chords

F	F–A–C
Fm	F–A♭–C
F7	F–A–C–E♭
Fdim	F–A♭–B
F+	F–A–C♯

F♯ or G♭ chords

F♯	F♯–A♯–C♯
F♯m	F♯–A–C♯
F♯7	F♯–A♯–C♯–E
F♯dim	F♯–A–C
F♯+	F♯–A♯–D

G chords

G	G–B–D
Gm	G–B♭–D
G7	G–B–D–F
Gdim	G–B♭–D♭
G+	G–B–D♯

G♯ or A♭ chords

A♭	A♭–C–E♭
A♭m	A♭–B–E♭
A♭7	A♭–C–E♭–G♭
A♭dim	A♭–B–D
A♭+	A♭–C–E

A chords

A	A–C♯–E
Am	A–C–E
A7	A–C♯–E–G
Adim	A–C–E♭
A+	A–C♯–F

B♭ chords

B♭	B♭–D–F
B♭m	B♭–D♭–F
B♭7	B♭–D–F–A♭
B♭dim	B♭–D♭–E
B♭+	B♭–D–F♯

B chords

B	B–D♯–F♯
Bm	B–D–F♯
B7	B–D♯–F♯–A
Bdim	B–D–F
B+	B–D♯–G

Important Note: A slash chord (C/E, G/B) tells you that a certain bass note is to be played under a particular harmony. In the case of C/E, the chord is C and the bass note is E.